A GIFT OF PROPHECY

The Phenomenal Jeane Dixon

A GIFT OF PROPHECY

THE PHENOMENAL JEANE DIXON

RUTH MONTGOMERY

WILLIAM MORROW & COMPANY
NEW YORK, 1965

Fifth Printing

Copyright © 1965 by Ruth Montgomery and Jeane Dixon

A condensed version of this book has appeared in
The Reader's Digest under the title *The Crystal Ball*

Published simultaneously in the Dominion of Canada
by George J. McLeod Limited, Toronto.

Printed in the United States of America.

Library of Congress Catalog Card Number: 65-21204

TO

All those who seek answers to the eternal mystery of life and who, recognizing that there is a Power greater than ourselves, find inspiration in the Biblical injunction: "Ask, and it shall be given you; seek, and ye shall find; knock, and it shall be opened unto you."

FOREWORD

WE Americans are accustomed to think of visions in terms of biblical lore, and to associate the city of Washington with power politics and faceless bureaucracy. It seems remarkable, therefore, to discover in this bustling New World capital a modern-day psychic whose visions apparently lift the curtain on tomorrow in much the same manner as did those of Old Testament prophets.

Because of this uncanny gift Jeane Dixon has become almost as much of an institution as the Pentagon, during the quarter century in which they have shared the national limelight. Both made their appearance in Washington early in the Second World War, and since then they have been approached by innumerable foreign dignitaries. From the Pentagon these overseas visitors sought dollars and armaments, from Mrs. Dixon a glimpse of the future; the foreign-aid money was dispensed with certain strings attached, but Jeane Dixon has declined to accept any remuneration for a talent which she believes God bestowed on her for a purpose. Devoutly religious, she will use her strange gift only for the benefit of others. She believes that if she were to take money she might lose this talent.

As a skeptical newspaper reporter I was unimpressed by these alleged powers until, as the years passed, the accuracy of her many forecasts began to forge an impressive chain of evidence. She was naming presidential slates long before delegates gathered in quadrennial convention to make the nominations. With regularity she was picking each White House winner a year in advance of his election. She not only foresaw death or downfall for certain world leaders but was able to pinpoint the time when these would occur. World-shaking events were sometimes foretold a decade ahead of time, and eventually they came to pass in the precise year that she had mentioned.

I first began writing yearly columns about Jeane Dixon's forecasts in 1952, simply as a change from the steady discourses on politics and world affairs. Gradually I became sufficiently impressed with the phenomenal accuracy of her predictions to be relieved when on occasion she missed. Had she always been right, some of her forebodings would have seemed too horrific for comfortable contemplation. I did not believe that President Kennedy would be assassinated. I refused to accept her pronouncement that Secretary of State Dulles would die in the spring of 1959. I declined to print her 1952 prophecy that serious race rioting would bloody our American streets in 1963 and 1964.

Conversely, Jeane made a few forecasts that failed to occur. She predicted that Red China would plunge the world into war over Quemoy and Matsu in October of 1958; she thought that labor leader Walter Reuther would actively seek the presidency in 1964. She blames herself for these errors, believing that she was shown correct symbols but misinterpreted them. A noted psychologist who is an authority on extrasensory perception has an entirely different explanation, which is discussed in this book.

For those who shudder at some of the awesome "coming events" that Jeane feels have already cast their shadows before them, it is comforting to remember that she is not infallible; but her record of accuracy is such that the burden of that proof must rest upon future historians. In certain cases the names and places have been changed in order to protect the people involved, and avoid any possible invasion of privacy.

Certainly there is no intent to embarrass anyone, living or dead.

Since I am without psychic talent and can see only my own distorted image reflected in a crystal ball, I have simply attempted to set forth, with as much reportorial accuracy as possible, the amazing story of Jeane Dixon.

R. M.

Washington, D.C.

CHAPTER

I

It was a bright, crisp day in late November. The luncheon had been scheduled several weeks in advance, and as the three fashionably dressed women entered the Presidential Dining Room of the Mayflower Hotel the orchestra leader smiled and nodded in recognition. The maître d'hôtel seated them at a reserved table and ceremoniously presented the menu cards. Mrs. Harley Cope, widow of a rear admiral, and Jeane Dixon, Washington's famous seeress, ordered eggs Florentine. Mrs. Rebecca Kaufmann, a native Washingtonian, mentally counted calories and searched her conscience before choosing the rich lobster salad.

When the food arrived, Mrs. Cope and Mrs. Kaufmann immediately began to eat, while carrying on an animated conversation. Mrs. Kaufmann, noticing that Jeane did not touch hers, exclaimed, "Child, why aren't you eating? Surely you don't have to watch your weight, with that twenty-two-inch waistline of yours!"

The attractive brunette leaned back against her chair and closed her eyes. "Mrs. Kaufmann," she said, "I just can't. I'm too upset. Something dreadful is going to happen to the President today."

"Today? What are you saying?" the motherly dowager asked.

Jeane could only nod miserably, while Mrs. Cope explained, "Mrs. Dixon has been foreseeing a tragedy for President Kennedy very soon. She told me about it day before yesterday."

Mrs. Kaufmann, who has witnessed many griefs since she was born in turn-of-the-century Georgetown, patted Jeane's hand consolingly. "Don't worry about it, dear," she counseled. "What is going to happen will happen, and it does no good to anticipate trouble."

Sorrow shone in Jeane's blue-green eyes, and as she fought to maintain self-control she said, "Yes, the will of humanity cannot change the will of God."

At that moment the music of Sidney Seidenman's internationally celebrated orchestra ceased, and the conductor hastened to their table. Greeting the three women by name, he said, "Someone just tried to take a shot at the President!"

Mrs. Dixon murmured tonelessly, "The President is dead."

Sidney, whose dance bands have performed for White House soirées and debutante balls since the Herbert Hoover era, attempted to reassure the distraught ladies. "No, no, he isn't. He may not even have been struck."

"You will learn that he is dead," Jeane repeated in the same oddly detached voice.

Sidney rushed from the room but returned almost immediately to report that President Kennedy was only wounded. "I heard it on the radio," he said soothingly. "He's still alive, and they're giving him a blood transfusion."

Jeane gazed at him numbly. "The radio is wrong," she said with quiet finality. "President Kennedy is dead. I tried to send a warning to him, but no one would listen. Now it is too late."

Recalling her prophetic utterance, the orchestra leader

later told me: "Mrs. Dixon is a very sweet woman. I had heard that she sometimes has portents, or whatever you call them, but I'm not much of a believer in those things. I just felt that she was mistaken . . . but within a half hour we knew that she was right."

Halfway across Washington another luncheon was in progress. Lady West had stopped in at Kay Halle's historic red brick house in Georgetown to report on a motor tour of America from which she and Sir Michael West, chairman of the British Embassy's defense staff, had just returned.

"The one thing that most impressed us," Lady West began in clipped accent, "was the violence of feeling in your country. In Texas we were received with warmth and hospitality; yet everywhere we went we were simply staggered by the violent way in which you Americans argue politics. Now in England . . . "

The maid interrupted to announce that Mrs. Alice Roosevelt Longworth (the daughter of President Theodore Roosevelt) would like to speak to the hostess. With an apology, Kay stepped to the telephone, called a cheery "Hello," and listened with horror as her friend exclaimed, "Turn on your radio quickly. It has happened . . . as Jeane Dixon said it would."

Her hands beginning to tremble, Miss Halle switched on the nearest radio. A voice was booming: "We repeat, the President has been shot. We do not yet know how seriously he is wounded, but we are standing by at the Parkland Memorial Hospital, here in Dallas."

The date was Friday, November 22, 1963. Eleven hundred miles southwest as the crow flies, a zing of shots had punctuated the autumn air and an assassin's bullet found its mark with deadly precision. Kay Halle had reason to be even more horrified at the chilling news than most of the rest of America. A few weeks before the tragic event in Dallas, Kay, who is the daughter of Cleveland philanthropist Samuel Halle, had answered her doorbell and admitted Mrs. Dixon, who was in an agitated state.

"Please forgive me for running in this way," Jeane apologized, "but I know how close you are to the Kennedys. The President has just made a decision to go someplace in the South that will be fatal for him. You must get word to him not to make that trip."

As Kay tried to collect her thoughts, Jeane continued, "For a long time I've been seeing a black cloud hovering over the White House. It kept getting bigger and bigger, and now it's beginning to move downward. That means that the time is near. He will be killed while away from the White House."

Kay, who had only a casual acquaintanceship with Mrs. Dixon, tried to be polite, but stalled by saying, "If these things are predestined, there isn't much that we can do about them, is there?"

Jeane was not to be put off so easily. Curving her thumb and forefinger almost together, she said earnestly, "There is sometimes one tiny little moment in time when you can tip the scales and turn the event aside. You must warn him."

Kay Halle knew President Kennedy well. She had served on his Inaugural Committee and had conceived the idea of inviting the two hundred eminent award winners in the fields of art, science, and the humanities as special guests to his inauguration. It was she who subsequently persuaded him to recommend honorary American citizenship for Sir Winston Churchill and helped to prod the bill through Congress. She had visited Sir Winston many times at his country seat, Chartwell, and heard him intone, "I am an English-Speaking Union."

Now she regarded her caller with embarrassment. She had heard that Jeane was psychic, but she knew how foreign such interests were to the ebullient Kennedy clan. She also surmised that Jeane was not infallible. With a nervous laugh she asked, "How can I carry such a message to the President? Until now the people at the White House have considered me a reasonably sensible person. What would they think if I brought such a mystical warning as this?"

Jeane understood her reluctance. She had encountered such resistance before, but nevertheless she pleaded with Kay to convey the message. Kay finally agreed to do what she could, and Jeane, thinking that she had won her consent, departed in happier mood.

"I did turn it over in my mind, over and over and over," Kay ruefully told me afterward, "but I simply could not bring myself to deliver such a dreadful, nebulous warning. Frankly, I couldn't even convince myself that it was true, and knowing how brave and determined President Kennedy was, I realized that he would have been the last to give heed to such a warning. I subsequently discussed Jeane's warning with Alice Longworth, and we looked somewhat nervously at each other, but what could we do? We Americans simply haven't the capacity to embrace something like this. I knew that the Kennedys would consider it some kind of mumbo-jumbo. The President would have laughed at the mere suggestion of it."

Alice Longworth, musing about it later, said frankly, "I don't really believe in these things, but naturally I listen when people tell me about them. Everyone has a certain curiosity, I suppose."

Shortly after the President's assassination Kay Halle related the strange sequence of events to Ambassador G. Frederick Reinhardt during a dinner party at Mrs. Longworth's home. When she had finished, our envoy to Italy exclaimed in a shocked tone, "This is an incredible story!"

Actually the incredible story had its beginning eleven years earlier, in 1952. A misty rain was falling as Jeane entered St. Matthew's Cathedral for her morning meditation. For several days she had experienced an odd sensation of withdrawal—a condition that she had come to recognize as the forerunner of an important vision.

She remembers that she had deposited some coins for candles, and was preparing to kneel in prayer before a statue of the Virgin Mary, when the White House suddenly appeared in radiant brilliance before her. Almost immediately the numerals "1960" formed above it, and as she watched, a dark cloud spread from the numbers and "dripped down like chocolate frosting on a cake" over the White House and a man standing in front of it. The man, she recalls, was young, tall, and blue-eyed, with a shock of thick brown hair. An inner voice told her that he was a Democrat, and that the President elected in 1960 would meet with violent death while in office. As suddenly as the vision came it vanished, but the sense of worldly detachment remained with Jeane for three more days.

Four years later, while two reporters from *Parade* magazine were interviewing her about predictions, she abruptly skipped over the intervening years and declared, "A blue-eyed Democratic President elected in 1960 will be assassinated."

Startled by the bluntness of her words, the reporters suggested that they simply say he would "die in office."

"Say it as you like, but he will be assassinated," she replied. Her prediction appeared in the *Parade* issue of March 11, 1956, and Jeane's friends remembered it when John F. Kennedy won the upset victory of 1960. Her description of the man in the vision bore a disquieting resemblance to the President-elect. Moreover, Jeane continued to "see" the black cloud hovering above the White House.

In the summer of 1963, when little Patrick Kennedy lost his brief struggle for life, Jeane Dixon's telephone began to ring frequently. Lorene Mason, a Washington secretary, and other friends wanted to know whether the death of the President's three-day-old son could explain the dark cloud that she had for so long seen over the White House. Jeane had to reply in the negative.

"It cannot be," she explained, "because I still see a large coffin being carried into the White House. This means that the President will meet death elsewhere and his body will be returned there for national mourning."

Time passed, and Jeane busied herself with her real estate activities. She was also a volunteer worker for the Damon Runyon Cancer Fund, and in this capacity had presented checks for tens of thousands of dollars to U. S. and foreign ambassadors for cancer research abroad. One evening in late October 1963 she dined with Dr. F. Regis Riesenman, an eminent psychiatrist and researcher in parapsychology, at Duke Zeibert's restaurant, and he recalls, "Mrs. Dixon told me that she had had a vision in which she saw Lyndon B. Johnson's name being removed from the vice-presidential door. She said she had glimpsed the name of the man who would cause this to happen, and that although it had faded rapidly she noticed that it was a two-syllable word containing five or six letters. She was quite positive that the second letter was an *s*."

The day before Jeane dined with Dr. Riesenman she had telephoned me and breathlessly declared, "I have some information which won't wait for your New Year's column on my predictions. It's terribly important! May I come right over?" She arrived by taxi a few minutes later and, as she rushed into the house, said, "I've had a vision. As plainly as you see me now, I saw someone removing Lyndon Johnson's name from the door of the vice-presidential office. Is there a plaque by his door that says 'Vice-President'? There must be, because I saw the sign being removed, but not by him. Then I saw an unknown man, and his name flashed past my eyes. It was a two-syllable name with five or six letters. The second letter was definitely an *s,* and the first looked like an *o* or a *q,* but I couldn't be sure. The last letter ended with a little curve that went straight up."

Since the name of Billie Sol Estes, the Texas grain speculator, was then in the headlines, and some anti-Administration writers were trying to link him with his fellow Texan, Lyndon Johnson, I asked if she thought the name could be Estes. That name has two syllables, and the second letter was an *s.*

Jeane replied at once, "No, it couldn't be Estes, because the first letter of the name was definitely closed, like an *o* or a *q.* Besides, I get that the removal of Mr. Johnson's name from the door will not be of his own doing. It will be a circumstance beyond his control. I also see Lady Bird Johnson having some kind of trouble with her business affairs, although it will not be her fault. She, too, will be a victim of circumstances."

I asked if she had "seen" this curious event in her crystal ball, and she said, "No, this was a vision that appeared to me early this morning, just after I had risen from saying my prayers. As I always do on rising, I was standing at my window, facing the east and silently repeating the Twenty-third Psalm. I was not even thinking of government. Just as I said the words, 'Yea, though I walk through the valley of the shadow of death I shall fear no evil, for Thou art with me,' two black hands reached up and removed the plaque from the Vice-President's door. They were the hands of death. As the plaque disappeared, I saw the five- or six-letter name flash before me and knew that this man was causing it."

What Jeane so vividly described made little sense to me, but because she was so obviously stirred I tried to get more information from her. Reconstructing the vision, she said that she saw Lady Bird Johnson's name in the headlines, and that some transaction having to do with her business affairs would receive a great deal of unfavorable publicity, casting a shadow on Mr. Johnson's personal reputation, although not on his wife's.

"I simply wanted to alert you to what is going to happen," Jeane said, "because it will be very soon. It won't keep until you are ready to write the annual New Year's column about my predictions."

On Sunday, November 17, 1963, she had an engagement to dine with Mr. John Teeter, executive director of the Damon Runyon Memorial Fund, the Vicomtesse Fournier de la Barre of Paris, and Miss Eleanor Bumgardner at a favorite restaurant on the outskirts of Washington.

"Jeane picked me up in her car," Miss Bumgardner recalls, "and I sensed immediately that something was wrong. She seemed way out, as if her mind were elsewhere. She's usually an excellent driver, but that day she was creeping along at such a snail's pace that I finally asked her what was the matter."

She remembers that Jeane replied, "I just can't get my mind off the White House. Everywhere I go I see the White House with a dark cloud moving down on it. Something tragic is going to happen very, very soon."

Miss Bumgardner noticed that Jeane barely touched her food. When Mr. Teeter commented on the fact, Jeane gave up all pretense of eating. "I have never had anything overpower me like this vision," she said. "It's every place I look. Something dreadful is going to happen to our President—and soon!"

Eleanor Bumgardner is called "Lady" by her multitude of friends. The nickname was originally bestowed by her former employer, the late Supreme Court Justice Frank Murphy. More recently she had been working as a personal secretary to Mrs. Sargent Shriver, the President's sister Eunice. Three years earlier Jeane had told Lady Bumgardner, "It's very bad for Jack Kennedy to be running for President this year. If only he would wait eight years, for his own good alone! It will be disastrous for him at this time." Lady could not put that remark from her mind, or stop thinking of Jeane's odd behavior at the Sunday luncheon with Mr. Teeter and the vicomtesse, so on Monday she stopped in at the Dixon real estate office.

Jeane, seated at her desk, barely greeted Lady before exclaiming, "Dear God! In a very few days the President will be killed. I see his casket coming into the White House. I hope that Kay Halle reaches him in time to tell him not to make that Texas trip."

Miss Bumgardner recalls her own relief on hearing that Jeane had arranged for another person to warn the President directly, for she had felt as reluctant as Kay Halle to carry such a macabre message to a member of the Kennedy family.

On Wednesday, November 20, Jeane attended a business luncheon with Mrs. Cope and Charles Benter, the organizer and long-time leader of the U. S. Navy Band, who had participated in fourteen inaugural parades along Pennsylvania Avenue. Now retired from active service, Mr. Benter was working at the James L. Dixon Company, and Mrs. Cope was listing some of her properties with the realty agency. Jeane, ordinarily a keen participant in such real estate transactions, seemed not to be listening that day, and after Mr. Benter twice repeated something to her, she murmured, "I'm sorry, but I just can't hear what you say, because the President is going to be shot."

Mrs. Cope, thinking that she had misunderstood, asked, "Who did you say was going to be shot?"

"Our President. President Kennedy," Jeane lamented.

"Oh, don't say such a thing," admonished the admiral's widow.

Thursday Jeane literally paced the floor of her office. When David Greene, one of the salesmen, remarked that she seemed upset, she told him, "The President is going to be assassinated."

Alarmed because he had witnessed other manifestations of Jeane's prophetic talents, he cried, "Can't we do something about it?"

Jeane replied that she had asked Kay Halle to get word to President Kennedy to cancel his trip, but that he had gone to Texas anyway. "And now I see death rocking in his rocking chair. If only he could keep himself invulnerable to bullets for the next few days!"

The following morning Jeane went to Mass, as she does every morning of her life, and afterward met Mr. Benter for breakfast in a coffee shop near the office. As she slid into the booth beside the fatherly old veteran, she clasped his hand and sighed, "This is the day it will happen!" They looked helplessly into each other's eyes.

John Fitzgerald Kennedy, the vibrant young President, had but four more hours to live.

The death of John F. Kennedy was shattering to me, for he had been my long-time personal friend as well as my President. The full portent of Jeane's mysterious prophecy did not strike me, therefore, until I learned that Lee Oswald had been apprehended for the murder. Oswald! The name that Jeane had fleetingly glimpsed in her vision, as the black hands of death removed the vice-presidential plaque from the door! Oswald began with an *o*, and the next letter was *s*. It was a two-syllable name with six letters, and the last letter had a curve that "went straight up." Her eerie forecast concerning the President had come true in minutest detail.

But that was not all. A few weeks after Lyndon Baines Johnson took the presidential oath of office, a Senate committee launched an investigation into the influence peddling of Senate majority secretary Robert Baker, Mr. Johnson's former protégé. Insurance broker Don Reynolds swore that in order to sell a large life insurance policy to majority leader Johnson after his heart attack he had been pressured into buying useless advertising time on KTBC, the Austin television station owned largely by Lady Bird Johnson.

Jeane had foreseen that a transaction having to do with Mrs. Johnson's business affairs would receive unfavorable publicity, although she would not be personally to blame. No witness or senator insinuated that Mrs. Johnson had herself been a party to the pressure, but the President's own possible connection with it became a major issue in the 1964 campaign.

Jeane Dixon had scored correctly on every count.

Within three months of the assassination of President Kennedy Jeane's psychic attunement to unknown forces brought further disquieting news. To Kay Halle, Eleanor Bumgardner, and me she said, "The tragedies in the Kennedy family are not yet ended. I see another one soon, for another male member of the family."

On the morning of Friday, June 19, 1964, Mrs. Walter Stork telephoned Mrs. Dixon to talk of family problems. Mr. Stork, a distinguished government official who has served under every President since Calvin Coolidge and been decorated by Presidents Eisenhower and Kennedy, lay ill of Parkinson's disease. Doctors agreed that his condition was incurable, and although Mrs. Stork had hopefully arranged to have him transferred to a different hospital, she was trying to prepare herself to "accept God's will."

Her voice breaking, Mary Alice Stork told Jeane, "If anything happens to my beloved Walter, I'm going to ask that he be buried as close to President Kennedy in Arlington as possible, because he loved him so much."

Jeane said with a sigh, "Mary Alice, the tragedies in the Kennedy family are not ended. I see another one almost immediately."

"You mean the President's father?" Mrs Stork asked, thinking of the incapacitating stroke that the patriarch of the clan had suffered nearly three years before.

"No, no," Jeane replied. "This is the young senator. Mary

Alice, if you love the Kennedys so much, please warn them that Teddy simply must stay out of private planes for the next two weeks. Otherwise, something very, very serious will happen."

The next morning Mrs. Stork picked up the newspaper at her door and read the glaring headline. Senator Edward Kennedy had been gravely injured in the crash of a chartered plane which took the lives of his closest assistant and the pilot. Senator and Mrs. Birch Bayh had been less seriously injured than Ted Kennedy, whose back was broken. Mrs. Stork rushed to the phone and frantically dialed Jeane's telephone number. "Jeane, it has happened! Your premonition was right, as usual."

Jeane, who had not yet heard the news of the plane crash, listened quietly while Mrs. Stork read her the details. When she had finished, Jeane said only, "It was not a premonition. God showed it to me."

CHAPTER
2

THROUGH a curious chain of circumstances, it was a gypsy who awakened Jeane to the strange potential within herself. Borne Jeane Pinckert in a Wisconsin lumbering village shortly before the armistice that ended World War I, she moved as a child to California with her parents, Emma Von Graffee and Frank Pinckert.

Herr Pinckert, who brought his bride to America on a honeymoon, liked the New World so much that he had sold out his interests in Germany to return here. At the age of forty-five, having amassed a comfortable fortune, he retired and moved his family to Santa Rosa, California. He had long taken a lively interest in American Indians, and after developing a warm friendship with Luther Burbank, the world-renowned horticulturist, he also became fascinated by nomadic gypsies who roamed the countryside. One day, learning that a gypsy woman was encamped on Burbank's estate, he suggested that his wife take Jeane to see her. The encounter revolutionized the child's life. Recalling that meeting, Jeane still bubbles with excitement.

"The gypsy lady had a covered wagon with a stovepipe

jutting out of the canvas roof," she says. "Chickens poked their heads out of the wagon door, and a horse that was tied to a tree kicked and bounced wildly while we were there. The gypsy lived mostly out of doors, but she kept the ground spotlessly clean by sweeping it with a broom, and I remember that she pared her fingernails with a pocket knife."

The gypsy was telling a woman's fortune with cards as Mrs. Pinckert and her eight-year-old daughter arrived at the campsite. When Jeane's turn came she took the child's hands, turned them over, and gasped. "This little girl is going to be very famous. She will be able to foresee world-wide changes, because she is blessed with the gift for prophecy. Never have I seen such palm lines!"

The youngster had been taught by Indians who worked for her father to ride ponies bareback but had not yet gone to school. Tutored at home by her parents and a European governess, she spoke German better than English. Nevertheless she understood that the gypsy was warning her mother to "protect her from people" because of her unusual sensitivity.

"Look at her left hand," the gypsy marveled. "Here is a star of David, and with this double head line leading from it, she would need no other symbol in order to have the gift of prophecy. But look also at this! She has another star on the Mount of Jupiter [the mystic name for the hump at the base of the index finger], and in her right palm is this tremendous star that reaches out in all directions. I've never seen such a head line. It completely crosses the palm and wraps around the hand, with a half-moon on its outer cuff."

Noticing for the first time these unusual markings on her daughter's hands—markings which a Hindu mystic later told Jeane occur perhaps once in a thousand years—Mrs. Pinckert asked the significance of them.

"They mean," said the gypsy solemnly, "that this child will grow mightily in wisdom. The lines in the left hand are the blueprint of one's dreams and potential. Those in the right hand signify what you do with what God has given you. She is already developing fast."

The gypsy disappeared into her covered wagon and returned with a crystal ball. Handing it to Jeane, she said: "It's for you to keep. You will be able to meditate on this and see wonderful things in it, for the markings on your hands are those of a mystic." Jeane eagerly peered into the shining new "toy" and pictures began to form within it. Although television was unknown in those days, it was as if she were watching a TV screen.

"I saw great waves of blue water," she says, "and somehow realized that I was seeing the bay in a far-off land from which the gypsy originally came. I described what I saw, and she said it was just as she remembered it. Cupping my hands around the ball, I saw her reaching over a strange kind of cooking pot. I sensed danger and cried out that she must be careful not to scald herself. The next time that we returned for a visit her hands were bandaged. She said they were deeply burned from scalding water which she had upset while cooking."

And what was the reaction of Jeane's gently reared, German-born mother, on being told of her daughter's strange talent? Jeane shrugs. "Mother didn't seem to consider it unusual. She simply said that if God had given me that gift she wanted me to use it only for good on this earth."

The Pinckert offspring, reared in the cultured European tradition by wealthy parents, had a German nursemaid called "Mother Koosey," who ruled the children with a firm hand. But Jeane's life was most deeply influenced by her soft-spoken, aristocratic mother and her dominating father, who impressed upon the youngsters the need for having a purpose in life.

"Mother always said that we did not belong to her but to God," Jeane muses. "She felt that we were only entrusted to her care. Although she and Father were devout Catholics, Mother often remarked that no soul should be tied to one church because, no matter where we worshiped, the same Almighty Power guided each of us. She felt that it was her responsibility to see that we developed whatever talents were given to us at the time of our conception."

It was in that spirit that Mrs. Pinckert encouraged Jeane's "sixth sense." She had already realized that Jeane was different from her six other children. When barely able to talk, the child had toddled to the door one day and asked permission to play with "the letter trimmed in black." Puzzled, Mrs. Pinckert replied that there was no such letter, but ten days later a black-bordered letter arrived by boat from Germany, bringing the sad news that her father, Garhardt Von Graffee, was dead. A year later, while Mr. Pinckert was on a business trip to Chicago, Jeane told her mother, "Father will bring back a great big black and white dog." When he returned with a rare black and white collie, Mrs. Pinckert asked the little girl how she had guessed it, and Jeane replied that she had "seen" her father buying it.

One day her older brother Erny tossed Jeane into a haymow, and suddenly she exclaimed: "Oh, Erny, you're going to be a great athlete. I glimpsed you playing with a ball, and throngs of people were cheering." When their parents tried to discourage Erny from playing football, Jeane pleaded: "Please, please, let him play, because he's going to be very famous in sports and make you proud of him." Within the decade Erny Pinckert's name was to be inscribed as an All American in football's Hall of Fame.

For a time Jeane was inclined to use the crystal ball as a plaything. She naturally assumed that everyone could see pictures in it and that it was merely something to enjoy, like a kaleidoscope. It was Mrs. Pinckert who took care of it and sought to encourage Jeane's strange talent. Friends soon discovered the child's knack for predicting events, and after the

Pinckerts moved to Los Angeles even strangers began knocking on the door. Jeane was only nine years old when a woman introduced herself as Marie Dressler and said she was thinking of opening a boardinghouse because she was having no success as an actress. She asked Jeane to read for her, and as the little girl looked in her crystal ball it "lighted up like a Fourth of July sparkler." Describing what she saw, Jeane says: "Shooting off from this sparkler were hundred- and thousand-dollar bills, which I interpreted to mean that one day she would become a great star and earn a lot of money. I told her that she must give up the idea of a boardinghouse and devote all of her energies to acting."

"But I will starve to death if I do," Miss Dressler objected.

Jeane, whose parents had forsaken the Old World for the New, indignantly retorted: "Oh no! People in America don't starve. You must go on with your acting career."

After Marie Dressler's name began to flash on movie marquees across the nation, she often told people that if it had not been for little Jeane Pinckert she would have abandoned the theater. Jeane herself shrugs off the compliment, saying: "She would have been famous anyway, because that was her destiny. I could see it plainly. The crystal ball merely helped to guide her over the rough spots."

Years later Jeane had another dramatic encounter with an actress. During World War II she was having her hair set at Westmore's Beauty Salon in Los Angeles when Carole Lombard strolled in. Jeane of course recognized the glamorous movie star whose husband was Clark Gable. An operator introduced them and Jeane delightedly reached out to shake hands. As she did so she felt a warning vibration. Forgetting herself, she exclaimed: "Oh, Miss Lombard, you must not go anywhere by plane for the next six weeks."

The blonde actress smilingly replied that she was leaving almost immediately on tour, to promote the sale of war bonds. Jeane, who was also helping with the bond drive, realized the importance of Carole's mission but cautioned that she must travel only by automobile or train during the "danger" period.

The hair stylist who introduced them later told Jeane that after she left the salon Miss Lombard tossed a coin to see whether she should follow the unsought advice. She called heads, and the quarter landed tail up. The screen star flew to the Midwest a few days later and died in a plane crash.

Seeking to explain how she had sensed the impending tragedy, Jeane muses: "As I touched her hand I saw the death symbol over her. It was high above the ground. I saw life on the ground around her, and thus knew that if she would keep her feet on the ground she could elude danger. It was a sort of inner voice that said, 'Six weeks.' This voice comes to me frequently, and I always listen to it."

Jeane cannot remember when James L. Dixon first entered her life, nor can he recall their first meeting. Smiling reminiscently, she says: "It just seems that I have always known him. Although my parents were Catholics and Jimmy's father was a Methodist minister, our two families were good friends. He is much older than I, but I had secretly been in love with him since childhood. He married when I was only twelve years old, and it nearly broke my heart. No one knew this, least of all Jimmy. If they had, they would have regarded it merely as a schoolgirl crush."

To Jeane it was much more. Because she loved him so deeply she could not bring herself to see him after his marriage. Once she darted out of the Pig and Whistle, leaving her half-finished hot fudge sundae and a dollar bill, because she saw him entering the soda shop by another door. If she glimpsed him coming down the street she would hastily cross to the other side to avoid an encounter. Once a friend, suspecting her affection, loudly announced to the wealthy group summering at Newport Beach, California, that Jimmy Dixon had been killed. Her heart in her throat, Jeane went to a pay booth at a nearby drugstore and called the Dixon Chevrolet agency in Los Angeles. Jimmy himself answered the telephone. His deep, rich baritone voice was unmistakable, and she silently replaced the receiver. The man she loved was still alive.

On Jeane's sixteenth birthday Mr. Pinckert bought her an automobile, as was his custom with each of his children. As she slipped behind the wheel a vision flashed before her eyes, and she confided: "Father, when little Evelyn is sixteen she'll ask for an airplane instead of an automobile, and you'll get it for her. I can see her shooting out into the air in some strange way, too, without the airplane."

Herr Pinckert chuckled at this fantasy. Neither Jeane nor any of his other children had evinced any interest in planes. Nevertheless, on Evelyn Pinckert's sixteenth birthday she requested and received an airplane of her own. She became one of America's best-known aviatresses; made parachute jumps in the manner that her older sister had foreseen; and became the only woman ever engaged by U.S. military forces to teach aerobatics to army fliers.

CHAPTER

3

JEANE DIXON fascinates investigators of psychic phenomena because her precognition reveals itself through so many different channels. Sometimes she merely "tips the fingers" of a person and seems instantly to know what the future holds for him. She can often pinpoint events in the past and future for people she has never seen, merely by learning the date of their birth. Her most frequent revelations come through perusal of the crystal ball, but the forecasts to which she herself attaches the greatest significance have come through unsought visions.

Because I am without psychic ability and these phenomena are simply fascinating mysteries to me, I asked Jeane to discuss the different approaches and explain how she learned to interpret the symbols she so dramatically describes. This is her reply:

"As a small child, seeing visions which were not apparent to others, I described them to Mother Koosey, our German nursemaid. She would do her best to explain their meaning. A Catholic priest added another dimension, saying that whenever I saw purple and gold in visions I was tapping a highly spiritual realm. Visions are as different from the pictures in my crystal ball as day and night. When a vision begins to form everything changes, including the air around me. I seem no longer to be in the same atmosphere. I feel a peacefulness and a love that are indescribable. I stand alone, and nothing worldly can touch me. I feel that I am looking down from a higher plane and wondering why others cannot see what I am seeing.

"Unlike the pictures in the crystal ball, a vision is complete. The timing is right, for I have usually been prepared for it three days in advance. Occasionally I misinterpret the symbols in my crystal ball, but I never misinterpret a vision. Studying the crystal ball in order to find the answers that I seek for others draws a great deal of strength from me. Afterward I often feel debilitated. It is never like this with a vision. A vision fills you! I can only describe it by saying, 'My cup runneth over.' During this experience I'm so filled with the glory of God that I want to give everything to everyone. I feel that I will never be tired again, because I'm so full of strength. At such a time I feel that there is nothing in this world that I will ever want for myself.

"Once you have had a vision like that nothing in this world can awe you. You feel that at last you understand the word 'love.' You know what it is truly to worship God. You yearn to develop the talent that He has assigned you; to do His work on this earth. This doesn't mean that you are necessarily to go out and preach, but rather that you are to develop the special talents that He gave you. When you do that simple thing, you are thereafter filled with love. You do it automatically, and you want everyone else to experience this love you have felt.

"Suddenly you know the meaning of the words, 'Love thy neighbor' and 'Do unto others as you would have them do unto you.' But this does not mean that you can dump your problems on the Lord, without effort on your own part. I get very annoyed with men of the cloth who tell their flock to give their problems to the Lord. God gave us our own work to do. A janitor at our realty agency constantly neglected his work, and when we spoke to him about it, his reply invariably was that he would give the problem to the Lord. I finally told him that in that case I would give the Lord his pay check. We are put here to prove our own worth."

Describing how the crystal ball works for her, Jeane said: "In meditating on the crystal ball, I must try to pull out of it the life of another person. This takes a great deal of strength from me, because I must find that individual's color channel and often take on his ailments before I know that I am on the right course. It is the same with tipping the fingers. That person's sorrows or physical disabilities frequently become my own, and I am therefore depleted."

To illustrate, Jeane used several cases with which she knew I was familiar. The first incident occurred in my library, when I had invited her to tea to meet a beautiful young woman with whom I had become casually acquainted on a trip abroad.

When Mona learned that I was from Washington, she asked if I knew the Jeane Dixon of whom she had heard so much. I told her I was writing a book about Jeane, and she begged me to introduce her the next time she visited Washington.

I knew nothing about Mona except that she was beautiful, gay, and intelligent. Jeane had never heard of her, but after shaking Mona's hand she abruptly sank onto my Venetian couch and said, "My dear, you have a heart condition that could cause you some trouble if you are not careful. You must take care not to overstrain or overdo." Mona said nothing, and I thought Jeane had made a serious error. Obviously this vibrant young woman had nothing wrong with her. The ensuing pause was embarrassing for me, but evidently not for Jeane, who in a moment continued: "You tire easily. Some-

es you feel that you simply don't have the strength to go
."

While I was wondering how Jeane could say this about such an animated person, Mona said, "Mrs. Dixon, you are incredibly right. The doctors have told me that I have a heart condition, and sometimes I think that I don't have the strength even to draw the next breath."

Astonished, I protested: "But, Mona, you are always the gayest person in a group. You're bouncing with energy."

She shook her head. "It's an act. As I was riding over here today in a car, I wondered whether I could make it without lying down in the seat. I never know where the next breath of energy is coming from."

Concerned at this revelation, I jumped up and said: "Here, I'll get you a pep pill immediately—"

Jeane almost shouted: "She must never have a pep pill, never! If Mona took even one it might be the end for her. She must take liquid cod-liver oil every day and conserve her energy, but she must never, never take pep pills. For her, they could be fatal."

Later Jeane said to me: "Remember Mona? The moment I shook hands with her, my own heart began skipping beats. I felt that the blood was leaving my body, and I was so limp that I had to sit down quickly, in the first available spot, which was on the sofa beside her. I was utterly drained because I had taken on her vibrations. I had no energy and my heart was behaving strangely, so it was simple for me to diagnose her trouble."

A few weeks after the episode with Mona, another friend named Marta spent the evening with me. She seemed in a rather desperate state. After a brief period of marriage she had left her husband for logical reasons. He was under the care of a psychiatrist, and she was leading a successful and happy life in another city. Now she was on the brink of returning to her husband, although she kept saying that she did not want to.

"Why do I consider going back to him?" she asked me repeatedly. "I know that it will be the same thing all over again, yet he keeps begging me to come, and I feel that if I don't I will always hate myself for being a coward. But it won't work. I know it won't."

We discussed her problem endlessly. At last, knowing that I was unqualified to advise her, I telephoned Jeane to ask if she would meditate on Marta. I told her only Marta's birthday and the fact that she was wondering whether to return to the husband whom she had left. Although tired, Jeane agreed to do so provided Marta would meditate simultaneously. My friend went into the bedroom and knelt beside the bed. In a half hour Jeane telephoned to say:

"Ruth, I have picked up your friend's vibrations. She was suffering some pain in the intestinal region a few minutes ago, which I believe is a chronic condition caused from nervous strain. Your friend will go back to her husband no matter what you or I say, because she is being drawn like a magnet. It would be better for her if she could break it off now and forge a new life for herself, but she is unable to do so at this time. This magnet that is drawing her back is stronger than she is. She has unfinished business there, and until she has satisfied herself that she has done everything she can, no logic can stop her from completing that cycle of her life."

I delivered Jeane's message, and Marta confirmed that she had suffered pain in the intestinal region while she knelt beside the bed. This was not unusual, she added, because she had similar ones every morning. She also agreed that the pull she felt was like a magnet. Shortly afterward she returned to her husband and at last report was miserably unhappy.

The other case that Jeane gave as an example of her use of the crystal ball was that of my husband's sister, Rhoda Montgomery, for whom I had requested a reading, though she was a thousand miles away. Jeane was given her birthday but seemed stymied in her attempts to find Rhoda in her crystal ball. At last she admitted defeat, saying: "In the place where she should be, I keep getting a woman who was married many years ago—her marriage was chaos—and yet I know that your sister-in-law is a maiden lady."

I told her, then, that Rhoda had been married many years before for a brief period but had resumed her maiden name following the divorce. After that, information about Rhoda's past and future, including the fact that she had undergone a major operation, poured forth.

The fact that Jeane seemingly must assume these physical sufferings of others in order to pick up their vibrations, is one reason why she must refuse the requests of thousands who pleadingly write for appointments. It also explains why Jimmy Dixon, who is a highly successful businessman, insists that his wife work in his office. In that way he can keep an eye on her activities and provide her with a legitimate excuse when overzealous friends and strangers beg for readings. Jeane otherwise finds it almost impossible to say no.

In giving readings Jeane sometimes offers a worn deck of cards, which she asks the subject to shuffle and cut. Then she holds them in her own two hands but does not look at the faces of the cards. The deck, in fact, is not even a complete one, so I asked her the significance of this.

Her face relaxed in a soft smile. "The sweet old gypsy gave me those cards when I was eight years old, and because she blessed them they carry good vibrations. I don't know a single thing about telling fortunes with cards. I simply have a person hold them so that I can pick up his vibrations. It sometimes helps me to pull out his channels." After a moment she added: "I keep that worn-out old deck carefully wrapped in a handkerchief, because I just loved that gypsy!"

My next question concerned her knowledge of astrology. Why did she ask the day of a person's birth but not the year? With a whimsical smile, she confessed: "I don't do astrology. I could if I wanted to, because I was taught it by a Jesuit priest while in my teens, but it takes too much time.

People sometimes volunteer the hour and the year of their birth, but I don't ask for it. I merely want the month and day, because it makes it easier to find them in my crystal ball. You see, the ball represents the world or the year, depending on what I am seeking.

"It takes much strength and time if I have to look all over the crystal ball for the person's channel, but if I know that he was born in January or February, I look toward the front of the ball for him. If it was June or July, I will find him toward the middle; if November or December, toward the back of the ball. It's as simple as that."

Simple for Jeane Dixon, perhaps!

How does she do it? Jeane herself sees nothing eerie or uncanny about her talent. As matter-of-factly as if she were discussing a soprano's ability to hit high C, she says: "There are many varieties of gifts, but the same Spirit. There are varieties of service, but the same Lord over all. There are many forms of work, but the same Almighty Power above us, no matter what our language or religion. In each of us the Spirit is manifested in a particular way, for a purpose which He has designed for us. One person has the gift of wise speech. Another, by the same Spirit, can put the deepest knowledge into writing. Another has faith, another the gift of healing, another the gift of prophecy. All of these gifts are the work of one and the same Spirit. They are predetermined by God at the moment of our conception and are ours to develop for the good of others."

Jeane eats almost no meat. Her diet is composed primarily of vegetables, fruits, and juices. She never drinks or smokes, and before going to Mass each morning she stands at her bedroom window, facing east, while repeating the Twenty-third Psalm.

Such abstemious ways were common to many of the great seers and psychics of the ages, but this does not suggest that anyone can develop Jeane's gift by duplicating her habits. As she herself stresses, each of us has special talents which are ours to utilize to the fullest extent possible.

Few could hope, for instance, to duplicate the feat that she performed late in 1956. During the course of a newspaper interview a reporter asked for a forecast about Jawaharlal Nehru, who had then been Prime Minister of India since 1947. Jeane consulted her crystal ball and replied that he would be succeeded within approximately seven years by a man whose name would begin with the letter *s*. On May 27, 1964, death claimed the great Indian leader, and Parliament chose as his successor Lal Bahadur Shastri. Shastri's name, as foreseen slightly more than seven years before, did indeed begin with an *s*.

CHAPTER

4

In the years immediately preceding our entry into World War II, James L. Dixon and his partner, Hal Roach, owned the largest Chevrolet distributorship in the world. Roach was a renowned Hollywood producer, and a picture of the child stars in his popular "Our Gang" comedies appeared on the reverse side of the firm's business cards. Through his automotive connections, Jimmy had developed warm friendships with such industrial greats as Alfred P. Sloan, Jr., and William Knudsen. Another of his friends was Arthur Brisbane, and whenever the famous Hearst columnist came to California he wired ahead to Jimmy, who would meet him for breakfast at the Biltmore Hotel. After Brisbane finished his daily column, he and Dixon would tour the countryside together or call on publisher William Randolph Hearst at his fabulous estate, San Simeon.

Jeane Pinckert was meanwhile living in an entirely different world. In addition to her strange mystical talent, she combined a lovely mezzo-soprano voice with acting ability. At the age of twenty-one she played the supporting role of Mary Magdalene in *The Life of Christ* at the Hollywood

Bowl. On opening night her backstage dressing room was flooded with congratulatory telegrams and flowers, but she looked in vain for any word from Jimmy Dixon. She had not seen him in several years but she somehow thought that her well-publicized stage debut would come to his attention and he would remember her.

Jeane's next role at the Hollywood Bowl was as a lady-in-waiting in a production of Shakespeare's *Midsummer Night's Dream*. The director was Max Reinhardt, a friend of her father's. Jeane will never forget the costume she wore the day that publicity pictures were to be taken. Her gown was of gossamer yellow organza, tightly belted at the waist above a sunburst-pleated skirt, with which she wore black gloves, black high-heeled pumps, and a gold sunburst pin belonging to her mother.

Because she was running behind schedule she did not take time to change her frock or remove her make-up before joining friends in their box at the Hollywood track. The first race was already in progress, and when their horse ran out of the money the friends asked Jeane to place their bets on the second race "for luck." She had never before been to a betting window, but she memorized their choices and was mentally repeating them to herself as she pushed through the crowd. Suddenly she bumped headlong into Jimmy Dixon, who stared admiringly at the vision in yellow and exclaimed: "My, how the little girl has grown up!"

Intent on her chore, she scarcely nodded at the man who had once caused her to dodge across streets. This time it was Jimmy whose heart palpitated, and to his companion, Bert Northrup, he murmured dazedly: "That is the future Mrs. Dixon." Northrup could only stammer his surprise.

The same evening he telephoned her at home and after mentioning that he was now divorced asked if she would have dinner with him and his mother the following night. Jeane had known and loved Jimmy's mother since childhood and she hesitated only a moment before accepting the invitation. Before dinner was half finished Jimmy had made dates with Jeane for every evening that week and the next.

It was a whirlwind courtship, carefully chaperoned by Mrs. Dixon. Within five weeks they were married, but not before Jeane had twice returned Jimmy's five-carat diamond engagement ring and accepted it again at his mother's urging. It was not easy for a devout Catholic like Jeane to marry a divorced man, even one whom she had adored for nearly as long as she could remember. "Mother loved Jeane like a daughter—no, much more than a daughter," Jimmy recalls. "When we finally were married, Mother said she had waited a long time for such a joyous occasion. She knew that Jeane was right for me."

The wedding took place in San Diego. Jeane's girlhood chum, Mildred Kadlec, who was later to become her sister-in-law by marrying Erny Pinckert, handled the details and at the last minute hurried out to buy a substitute wedding ring, when the platinum band which matched the engagement ring proved too small.

The adjustment to marriage with Jimmy was not an easy one. No longer did she have time for daily voice lessons, stage roles, polo matches, and horseback riding. Jimmy, a golfer and businessman, was a stern taskmaster who expected her to be at his beck and call. His mother was still the matriarch of the house into which Jeane moved, and she continued to sit at the head of the table, with Jimmy opposite her. Jeane, finding her own place at one side, frankly liked the idea of a mother-in-law who could take the place of Mother Koosey in her life. She herself was untrained to manage the household, and the two women became so devoted that when the elder Mrs. Dixon died she left her estate to Jeane rather than to her own children.

The war in Europe had already begun when Jeane became a bride, and America was in a fever of preparedness. Jimmy, a specialist in automotive supplies, went to Detroit to work on defense projects, and while he and Jeane were living at Dearborn Inn she met an elderly blind man, a fellow tenant, to whom she began taking fresh-squeezed carrot juice and cod-liver oil "for his eyes."

Although she was a volunteer worker with Bundles for Britain, she also found time each morning to read the newspapers to the old gentleman, who was a friend of Henry Ford's. Dearborn Inn was across the road from Greenfield Village, the miniature early American town which the automotive pioneer had reconstructed, and Jeane often strolled through its streets with Mr. Ford. On one such excursion, when Mr. Ford was worrying aloud about some family strife, Jeane told him that he would outlive his only son, Edsel. Naturally he did not believe her, but this was to be. Mr. Ford chuckled at her absurdity when she said her crystal ball had shown her that a several-year gap would occur in Ford's assembly-line production of passenger cars, but within a year the tools of war occupied all motor assembly plants and private-car production ceased.

The war was pressing closer to our shores, and Jimmy traveled frequently between Detroit, Chicago, and New York. One morning while Jeane was meditating with her crystal ball she "saw" a plane go into a flaming crash. When Jimmy came home that afternoon to pack for a flight to Chicago, Jeane told him of the vision and warned that he must take the train instead. Jimmy demurred, and for the first time in her life she stamped her foot in frustration. Recalling that long-ago incident, Mr. Dixon says ruefully: "Like most husbands, I take the advice of my wife even though I don't like to have her think so. Sometimes I walk out of the house, still insisting on my own way, but when a man and wife are in love, he pays her heed. I did not fly that day." The plane on which he had held a ticket crashed just outside Chicago, killing all passengers on board.

December 7, 1941, brought double tragedy to Jeane and Jimmy Dixon. Scarcely had they learned of the sneak attack on Pearl Harbor when the telephone brought word that Jimmy's beloved mother had died of a heart attack on hearing the news. A few weeks after their return from California, Jimmy, who had served overseas with the 13th Aero Squadron in World War I and was now beyond military age, volunteered as a dollar-a-year man. Promptly assigned by the War Department to handle real estate acquisitions for depots and warehouses, he flew on to Washington and Jeane followed.

By the time Jeane arrived in the nation's capital it was bedlam. Long lines formed for restaurant service, and housing was at such a premium that hotel rooms could be retained for only three nights in a row. The Dixons, who had left behind their landscaped home and swimming pool in Los Angeles, now shuttled back and forth from one hotel to another. They settled at last in an apartment, and Jeane plunged into war work. So acute was her sensitivity that she had to turn down an invitation to become a Gray Lady, because she invariably took upon herself the sufferings of hospital patients and became physically ill, but she volunteered her services to the Home Hospitality Committee, which had been organized by local society women to provide recreation for servicemen and convalescents from army and navy hospitals.

Mrs. Martin Vogel, the chairman of the committee, gave frequent parties in her spacious mansion for the uprooted soldiers and sailors. Most of the embassies also opened their doors for entertainment of the men in uniform, and wives of senators, congressmen, cabinet officers, ambassadors, and government officials rotated as assistant hostesses. Jeane was a sensation from the start. Doing what she knew best, she began giving "readings" for servicemen, who eagerly queued up to hear what their future held. Mrs. Vogel, in recalling those anxious days, says of Jeane:

"She was always a great asset at the parties. The servicemen looked forward to being with her, and she especially inspired the amputees, many of whom had given up hope for a normal future. Jeane also spent much time at army and navy hospitals, going from ward to ward to cheer the convalescents. Our Home Hospitality parties included many celebrities. I remember honoring General and Mrs. Jimmy Doolittle, Myrna Loy, Robert Montgomery, and organist Virgil Fox at one gathering, but whenever I asked the servicemen which celebrities they most wanted to meet, they almost invariably said, 'Jeane Dixon.' They felt that Jeane was helping them to know themselves."

Pretty, blonde Patricia Parker, a junior hostess at the parties, remembers that, when soldiers sometimes complained about being sent to fight on foreign soil, "Jeane encouraged them by saying that this was their God-given opportunity to show America what they could do for it. They invariably sat up a little straighter when she said that, and threw their shoulders back."

Jeane's ever recurring slogan in those days, according to Patricia and others who worked with her, was: "It's not what your country can do for you; it's what you can do for your country." Her slogan found its way into print in the *Army Journal* of 1946, and in only slightly revised form became the stirring rallying cry of John F. Kennedy's inaugural address in 1961. "Ask not what your country can do for you," JFK phrased it, "but what you can do for your country."

Jeane particularly tried to help the amputees and the wounded realize that life was worth living. Of a paraplegic veteran Patricia Parker says, "He told me he would rather see Jeane Dixon than all the famous movie stars put together, because she gave so much of herself. Jeane literally helped these men come back to life by encouraging them and helping them to find their niche in life. By touching their fingertips she was able to discover latent talents which they could develop and utilize. Twenty years later she was still receiving letters from many of them, thanking her for instilling them with courage when they needed it most."

Sometimes at Home Hospitality parties Jeane read for legislators, diplomats, and other dignitaries, who to show their appreciation would donate money to the committee, since Jeane never accepted anything for herself. Before Patricia married Grayson Headley in 1946, Jeane read for her fiancé and foresaw that he would have an illness which would be extremely difficult to diagnose. She warned them both that when this time came he must immediately secure the best possible medical attention or it would be too late.

Eighteen years later Mrs. Headley recalls Jeane's prophecy as if it were yesterday, saying: "About five years before my husband's death, he was told that he had lymphosarcoma, a deadly cancer of the glands that takes one's life more quickly than leukemia. The doctors gave him no more than a year to live, but they were wrong. Four years later he began complaining of pain in his throat and visited several physicians. Each one sent him home with a prescription for antibiotics and the assurance that nothing was seriously wrong. When he finally had a biopsy it was too late. He had cancer of the larynx, and despite an operation he passed away six months later. An autopsy showed that he had never had lymphosarcoma, which had been a mistaken diagnosis. Jeane was right."

Jeane's fame as a seeress was spreading throughout Washington, and others were clamoring for her services. One evening while reading for guests at a charity party at the Sulgrave Club, Jeane touched the fingertips of Vice-President Harry S. Truman and prophesied: "You will become President through an act of God."

Another guest that evening was Eric Johnston, former president of the National Chamber of Commerce, who had once been talked about as a possible Republican presidential contender. Johnston asked Jeane whether he would receive an appointment from President Roosevelt, and after consulting her crystal ball she replied that though he would not get the governmental appointment he sought, he would accept another high post having to do with the motion picture industry. Mr. Johnston laughed out loud, but a few months after FDR's death he was offered the presidency of the Motion Picture Association of America, a position which he held for eighteen years until his death in 1963.

CHAPTER

5

FRANKLIN DELANO ROOSEVELT was not the first wartime President to summon a psychic to the White House at a time of national peril. Eighty-two years before petite Jeane Dixon took her crystal ball to the presidential office, by invitation, Abraham Lincoln had heeded the urgings of his wife and sent for a gently reared young medium named Nettie Colburn (later Maynard).

Like Mrs. Dixon, Miss Colburn was an amateur who discovered her psychic abilities by chance and accepted no money for the talent which she felt that God had bestowed on her. However, Jeane is not a trance medium and is therefore acutely aware of what is going on around her when she seemingly foresees future events by means of visions, crystal ball, or vibrations.

Miss Colburn's role as unofficial adviser to the presidential family began in December 1862, when Mary Todd Lincoln attended a séance at the Georgetown home of Cranston Laurie, a statistician with the Post Office Department. Also present that evening were the Hon. D. E. Somes, a former congressman from Maine; Thomas Gales Foster, an official at the War Department; the Rev. John Pierpont; a chief clerk in the Treasury Department; Mrs. Elvira M. Depuy of Washington; the Lauries and their daughter, Mrs. Belle Miller. Mrs. Lincoln was so impressed by what she heard and saw that she invited Miss Colburn to hold a séance for the President, and the first meeting with Abraham Lincoln occurred a few days later in the Red Room of the White House. An account of this and subsequent séances is to be found in several books on file at the Library of Congress, which are available for public perusal. Although I naturally cannot vouch for the facts about the Lincoln séances, which allegedly occurred while President Lincoln was heavily oppressed by Civil War decisions, the following material is quoted from the testimony of various witnesses as recorded in those books.

Mr. Lincoln entered the Red Room after the others had assembled, and on being introduced said kindly: "So this is our little Nettie, is it, that we have heard so much about?"

Miss Colburn then went into trance, and another voice reportedly talked through her for more than an hour, tracing the history of the nation and winding up with an impassioned plea for the issuance of the Emancipation Proclamation. A witness recorded: "The President was charged, with the utmost solemnity and force of manner, not to abate the terms of its issue, and not to delay its enforcement as a law beyond the opening of the year; and he was assured that it was to be the crowning event of his Administration and his life; and that while he was being counselled by strong parties to defer the enforcement of it, hoping to supplant it by other measures and to delay action, he must in no wise heed such counsel, but stand firm to his convictions and fearlessly perform and work and fulfill the mission for which he had been raised up by an overruling Providence."

Those present spoke of "the majesty of the utterance, the strength and force of the language, and the importance; and seemed to realize that some strong masculine spirit-force was giving speech to almost Divine commands." While standing in front of the President, Miss Colburn regained consciousness and stepped back in confusion, not remembering where she was. The President, with folded arms, was regarding her intently. A gentleman present asked in a low tone: "Mr. President, did you notice anything peculiar in the method of address?"

Lincoln raised his body as if shaking off a spell, glanced significantly at a full-length portrait of Daniel Webster hanging above the piano, and replied: "Yes, and it is very singular; very." Somes asked whether any pressure had indeed been brought to bear on the President to defer enforcement of the Emancipation Proclamation, and Lincoln replied: "Under these circumstances that question is perfectly proper, as we are all friends. It is taking all my nerve and strength to withstand such pressure."

While the men continued talking, Lincoln laid his hand on Nettie's saying: "My child, you possess a very singular gift; that it is of God, I have no doubt. I thank you for coming here tonight. It is more important than perhaps anyone present can understand." On January 1, 1863, President Lincoln issued the Emancipation Proclamation.

In early February of that year Mrs. Lincoln sent word that she would like to bring some friends to the Lauries' for another séance. The President had not expected to go along but at the last moment did so. Among others present were Colonel Simon P. Kase of Philadelphia, ex-Congressman Somes, and a major who accompanied the President.

At the beginning of the trance, while Mrs. Belle Miller played the piano, a "spirit force" allegedly lifted it off the floor. Lincoln, Somes, Kase, and the major seated themselves simultaneously on the piano to try to hold it down, but it continued to "rise and fall in time to the music." When one of the men remarked that no one would believe them about the piano, Lincoln wittily observed: "You should bring such a person here, and when the piano seems to rise, have him slip his foot under the leg and be convinced by the weight of evidence resting upon his understanding."

One of Nettie Colburn's "spirit controls," named Dr. Bamford, then took over and told Mr. Lincoln that a very precarious situation existed at the front where General Hooker had just taken command. The voice said the army was totally demoralized, regiments were stacking their arms, refusing to obey orders, and threatening a general retreat to Washington. Everyone present seemed surprised by such talk except the President, who said to the unconscious form of Miss Colburn: "You seem to understand the situation. Can you point out the remedy?" The so-called Dr. Bamford replied: "Yes, if you have the courage to use it." "Try me," Lincoln smilingly replied.

The voice told him to go in person to the front, taking his wife and children with him and leaving behind all dignitaries and all pomp. He was told to resist the pleas of high officials who would want to accompany him, and to take as few aides as possible. "Avoid high grade officers, and seek the tents of the private soldiers," the trancelike voice of Nettie instructed. "Inquire into their grievances, and show yourself to be what you are—the father of your people."

Lincoln responded quietly: "If that will do any good, it is easily done." The "spirit control" assured him that it would unite the soldiers as one man, and that in order to curb insubordination in the Army of the Potomac he should spread the news of his impending trip to the front without delay.

After Miss Colburn emerged from trance, Laurie asked if army morale could possibly be as bad as depicted by the "control," and Lincoln replied gravely: "It can hardly be exaggerated." Indicating the major who had accompanied him, Lincoln said: "He has just brought dispatches from the front depicting a state of affairs pretty much as our friend has shown it; and we were just having a cabinet meeting regarding the matter when something, I know not what, induced me to leave the room and come downstairs. When I found Mrs. Lincoln in the act of coming here, I felt it might be of service for me to come; I did not know wherefore."

He added that Miss Colburn "certainly could have no knowledge of the facts communicated to me, nor of what was transpiring in my cabinet meeting prior to my joining this circle, nor of affairs at the front, nor regarding transpiring events which are known to me only, and which I have not imparted to anyone, and which have not been made public."

The next day's *Gazette* bore the headlines: "The President is about to visit the Army of the Potomac." The article mentioned that a gunboat was being prepared for the President, who would take his family to Fortress Monroe. He went to the front and was literally borne on the shoulders of enthusiastic soldiers. All rallied behind him, with grievances forgotten. Mrs. Lincoln confided to friends that, when her husband was besieged by congressmen and cabinet members who wanted to accompany the President and his family, she reminded him that if he was going to take the advice of spirits he should take all of it. Therefore no high-ranking officials were permitted to go along.

Historians record that Miss Colburn was summoned several times to the White House. On one such visit Mrs. Lincoln exclaimed: "Oh, Miss Nettie, such dreadful news! They are fighting at the front; such terrible slaughter, and all our generals are killed and our army is in full retreat." News of the battle had not been made public, but Miss Colburn obligingly went into trance so that a control called "Wisdom" could report on the situation. "Wisdom" assured Mrs. Lincoln that her fears were groundless. While a great battle was indeed in progress, the voice said, Union forces were holding their own, and no generals had been injured or slain.

At that point the President, looking careworn, walked into the family quarters. Hearing what had just transpired, he asked for a repetition and "listened intently to every word for twenty minutes," while "Wisdom" told exactly how the battle was going and what the news would be by nightfall; that the battle was not disastrous and, though not decisive, would be a gain for the Union cause. Lincoln visibly brightened, and the next day's news confirmed the prediction.

During some reported séances with the Lincolns no observers were present, and therefore nothing is known of what took place. One evening, however, former Congressman Somes called on Miss Colburn to say that the President had asked that he bring her to the White House immediately. Lincoln and two military officers were waiting when they arrived. She was in trance for one hour. When she awakened she was holding a pencil and standing beside the President at a long table that contained a map of the Southern states.

"It is astonishing," Lincoln was saying, "how every line she has drawn conforms to the plan agreed upon." Then, noticing that she was now conscious, Lincoln said to Mrs. Lincoln and Somes: "Miss Nettie does not seem to require eyes to do anything."

On the way home from the White House that evening, Somes told Miss Colburn that the President had asked him and Mrs. Lincoln to remain at the other end of the room, so that they could not see the secret war map. Somes could observe, however, that Nettie was tracing lines on the map and that one of the officers occasionally resharpened her pencil.

The last time Nettie saw the President he wanted to know what her "friends" were saying now. He had just been reelected, and she told him: "What they predicted for you has come to pass, and you are to be inaugurated the second time. But they also reaffirm that the shadow they have spoken of still hangs over you."

Lincoln rather impatiently replied that he had received letters from mediums throughout the country warning him of a dire plot against his life. "But I don't think the knife is made, or the bullet run, that will reach it," he scoffed. "Besides, nobody wants to harm me."

Miss Colburn retorted that therein lay his danger—his overconfidence in his fellow men. With a sigh he replied: "Well, Miss Nettie, I shall live till my work is done, and no earthly power can prevent it. And then it doesn't matter, so that I am ready; and that I ever mean to be." Six weeks after his inauguration he was assassinated by actor John Wilkes Booth.

By the fall of 1944 articles about Jeane Dixon's prognostications had found their way into Washington newspapers, and several acquaintances asked her at veterans' parties whether she had yet had tea at the White House. When she said no they mysteriously hinted, "The President is interested in meeting you."

The following is her account of what happened.

One morning in November, shortly after Roosevelt's precedent-shattering re-election to a fourth term, Jeane Dixon answered the telephone in her apartment. A woman's voice, after assurance that she was speaking to Mrs. Dixon in person, said: "I'm calling for the President. We have heard so much about you, and the President would enjoy having a conversation with you. Are you free next Thursday at 11 A.M.?" Early on the appointed day a man called to confirm Jeane's morning appointment with the President.

She dressed with care, in a black suit designed for her by Adrian; it was trimmed with buttons shaped like crystal balls. With it she wore a matching pillbox hat and white gloves. The weather was warm for November, but because the crystal ball made her purse bulge she draped a silver fox fur piece over her arm to conceal it. The doorman hailed a cab for her, and in obedience to White House instructions she alighted at the northwest gate of the Executive Mansion on Pennsylvania Avenue. She gave her name to a guard, who had been alerted to expect her and waved her through. She walked up the winding driveway to the Executive West Wing and into the spacious lobby, where a vast round table caught her eye.

Tall, gray-haired William D. Simmons advanced to greet her, and after she had given her name he escorted her across the length of the room past a guard who said, "Hello, Jeane," and through a door behind Mr. Simmons' desk. They walked down a short corridor, through an anteroom, and into an oval office.

President Roosevelt, looking up from his desk, half raised his torso by his massive arms, flashed a warm smile, and said: "Good morning, Jeane. Thank you for coming." Wheeling himself toward the end of his desk, he shook her hand, and as he did so Jeane could almost feel the weight of the world pressing down on his broad shoulders. She took a chair at the corner of his desk, and they made small talk about the weather. Jeane, feeling "a wave of loneliness reaching out toward her," finally said: "Mr. President, it is wise to seek guidance sometimes, when one has a question in his mind."

Roosevelt sighed as he responded: "One's time is short, even at its longest. How much time do I have to finish the work I have to do?"

"May I touch your fingertips?" she asked. He thrust forward his big hand, and as she picked up his vibrations, she sought desperately to divert the conversation and avoid an answer. When he insisted on a direct reply, she said reluctantly: "Six months or less."

The room was still for a long moment. Then the President cleared his throat and said: "I've heard of some of the things you have discussed. I've been thinking about my decisions concerning Russia. In your discussions, what have you found?"

Jeane mentally noted how carefully he refrained from using the words "readings" or "psychic." To put him at his ease, she replied: "Mr. President, I don't have to look in my crystal ball or touch your fingers to answer that. Since I was fourteen years old I have been seeing in visions that America, France, England, and Germany must be allies before we will have real world peace. Germany should be on our side, helping to conquer Russia, instead of the other way around." War was then being waged on two fronts, and America, Britain, and France were tenuously allied with Russia against Germany and its Axis partners.

"Will we remain allies with Russia?" the President asked.

Shaking her head, Jeane said: "The visions show otherwise, but we will become allies again later on, against Red China."

The President reacted with a start. "Red China? China is not Red! We'll have no trouble with China. But I feel that we must be allied with Russia to maintain our world position and survive."

Looking intently at the pictures now forming in her crystal ball, Jeane said: "I see that China will go Communist and become our biggest trouble; Africa will be our next biggest worry in the foreign field."

The President disagreed, saying: "I don't anticipate any serious trouble with Africa, but I do with Russia. It is very important that we continue our alliance with Russia."

They talked a little longer; then, returning to his original question, Mr. Roosevelt asked slowly: "How much longer would you say, in years, that I have to complete my work?"

"Not years," Jeane corrected gently. "You can't measure it in years, Mr. President, but in months. Less than six months."

"Oh, that long?" he murmured, as if to himself. He turned to stare into space.

Recalling that uncomfortable pause, Jeane says: "I could see exactly what was going on in his mind. He was thinking, 'First things first,' and he was seeing files and files, stacks and stacks of papers. I could sense that he had felt a premonition of his own death. He was only seeking confirmation of the fact."

To interrupt his lonely thoughts, Jeane admired the figure

of an American eagle on his desk. Then they shook hands and he said in parting: "It was good of you to come."

In mid-January 1945, Jeane received a second call from the White House. A woman's voice asked: "Would you like to have a visit at the White House with the President?" An appointment was made for three days hence, again at 11 A.M., and Jeane arrived as before by cab. This time she noticed a group of men sitting in the chairs alongside the wall of the lobby opposite the round table, but they scarcely glanced at her as Mr. Simmons escorted her to the presidential office.

"Did you bring the ball?" President Roosevelt asked. There was an impish tilt to his cigarette holder as he greeted her.

"He felt as relaxed this time as he had been constrained before," Jeane muses. "But how his physical appearance had changed in those two months! His face was thin and haggard, and he looked as if fifty pounds had been dropped from his frame. But this time we met as old friends and fellow conspirators." As Jeane slipped the crystal ball from underneath the mink coat that Jimmy Dixon had given her for a wedding present, she and FDR exchanged knowing smiles.

"*Now* how much time do I have?" he asked, like a little boy who was impatient for his birthday presents.

Responding to his jovial mood, Jeane cupped her thumb and forefinger, leaving two inches between, and said: "That much."

The President, seeming to accept the fact that the end was approaching, nodded affably. "The time is short."

"Yes," Jeane reluctantly agreed, "shorter than we'd like to think."

Without waiting for an invitation, Mr. Roosevelt thrust out his right hand and asked: "How do you feel about some decisions I will have to make?"

"It is not how I feel personally," she corrected. "It's what I get spiritually and psychically. Many of the things I get that way are not what people want to hear."

As she touched his fingertips and closed her eyes, he pressed: "Are you sure that we will be allies with Russia in the future?"

Jeane reiterated her previous forecast that after the war's end the alliance would fall apart. "Eventually we will be allies with Russia against Red China," she said, "but that is more than a generation off."

"Then I'm not wrong about Russia?" he asked eagerly. "When all is said and done we will be with Russia, and Russia with us?"

"Yes, we will end up as allies," Jeane replied, "but our government will have changed by then. We are not always going to have a two-party system as we know it. But, Mr. President, we have a greater problem than Russia. America's far greater problem is our own racial situation. I have been shown this in a vision." He regarded her searchingly as she warned: "The White House must not pamper the colored people but rather help them to help themselves."

"I think the problem can be handled adequately," he replied with firmness.

"No, no," she contradicted. "We'll have bloodshed. I have seen it! The problem will grow beyond the reach of our government's wisdom. Mr. President, these are not my thoughts, they come through channels from another sphere. The will of humanity does not change the will of God. The racial situation will not be solved before 1980."

The President obviously did not agree, and for a time the air in the oval office seemed supercharged with tension. FDR foresaw no serious racial problem and frankly said so. Finally he brought the conversation back to the Soviets, saying: "The most important thing in the world is for us to get along with Russia and keep her as an ally."

At that moment Jeane saw a vision of Uncle Sam reaching

into another man's pocket, removing something from it, and giving it to a third country. "Oh, Mr. President," she exclaimed, "don't ever give anything away that doesn't belong to America. Don't give Russia half of anything that isn't ours to give!"

The President clenched both fists on the arms of his chair. "His thumbs were on the outside of each fist," Jeane recalls, "which I knew intuitively meant that he was sure he knew what was best and believed that whatever decision he had reached would be for the good of the nation. I felt that he was deeply dedicated to his country and that he had intuitive powers . . . but he was a sick man."

He seemed reluctant this time to see her go. When she held out her hand to say good-bye he covered it with both of his own. With a return of the sparkle to his eye, he told her: "Take good care of the ball."

Jeane returned the crystal ball to her big purse and said, *"Auf Wiedersehen."*

"God bless you," he replied. She never saw him again. Early in February he went to Yalta on one of the most closely guarded missions of the war. Together with Prime Minister Winston Churchill and Soviet Dictator Josef Stalin, FDR concluded a secret agreement which gave Russia domination over half of Germany, and much of its industry as reparations; the naval base of Port Arthur; the Kurile Islands; the northern part of Sakhalin and all islands adjacent thereto.

Did Jeane Dixon correctly foresee that an American President would "reach into another man's pocket" and hand over territory to Russia which was not ours to give? Certainly it was true that President Roosevelt had no more than six months to live after that first meeting with Mrs. Dixon in his office. On April 12, 1945, the heavily burdened President died of a cerebral hemorrhage in Warm Springs, Georgia.

CHAPTER
6

AMBASSADOR and Madame Wellington Koo were hosts at a large reception at Twin Oaks, the lovely hilltop estate which serves as the Chinese Embassy in Washington. It was a crisp evening in October 1946. The Western world clung to a tenuous peace, although President Truman had not yet issued a proclamation ending the hostilities, and ten Nazi war criminals had just been hanged. Guests clustered in small groups, as is their custom at embassy cocktail parties, to talk about the news of the day. One man, who considered himself something of an expert on world affairs, observed that it was a pity we had destroyed Germany while turning Russia loose on the free world.

"You're so right," another agreed. "Soviet Russia is even more of a menace to the United States than Germany was at its worst. We should have let them finish each other off. Mark my words, one of these days we'll have to fight Russia."

The wife of Ambassador Loy Henderson remembers the conversation particularly, for at that moment Jeane Dixon shyly interrupted: "I don't like to contradict you, sir, but I see America fighting Red China in the future, not Red Russia."

Mrs. Henderson, whose illustrious husband then headed Near Eastern and African Affairs for the State Department and had previously served as U.S. chargé d'affaires in Russia, regarded Mrs. Dixon in astonishment. "Why, China isn't Red," she exclaimed, "and with its rich cultural heritage it would never go for an alien ideology like Communism. The Chinese always keep to themselves."

Jeane's clear eyes regarded her imperturbably as she replied: "China will go Communist."

They all raised their eyebrows at that, Mrs. Henderson frankly admits, "because not one of us believed her that day." In 1948 Loy Henderson was appointed by President Truman as our ambassador to India, and during that tour of duty in New Delhi Mrs. Henderson had cause to remember Jeane's prophetic warning. On September 21, 1949, the Communists triumphantly proclaimed a People's Republic in Peiping, and in December Chiang Kai-shek evacuated his troops to the island of Formosa. The mainland of China was now Red.

One of the strangest predictions ever made by Jeane Dixon, who had never been outside of the continental United States, concerned the partition of India. Through frequent appearances at embassy parties she had developed friendships with numerous ambassadors, their wives and aides. One afternoon in 1945, at a reception given by Sir Girja Shankar Bajpai, the agent general for India, and Lady Bajpai, a military attaché introduced himself to her as Nawabjaba Sher Ali, and requested a private reading. Jeane received him the next day in her husband's business office and after consulting her crystal ball said that a partition of India would be announced within two years.

Shocked, the colonel exclaimed: "No, no, Mrs. Dixon. There will never be a partition of India."

Jeane unperturbedly declared that such a division would be announced on February 20, 1947, two years hence. Further, she said that the colonel himself would leave India to join the "other side," and would thereafter advance rapidly in his career. "Never!" he shouted. "My name in English means 'roaring lion,' and I will live out my days in an undivided India."

The Dixons continued to see the colonel from time to time at parties, and on the morning of February 20, 1947, he telephoned to twit her about her mistaken prophecy. Jeane confidently retorted that the day was not yet over. The next morning's newspapers headlined the partition announcement, and the Indian colonel, volunteering to eat crow, invited friends to a dinner party in Jeane's honor at nearby Fort Myer, in Virginia.

Automobiles were difficult to obtain in the early postwar years, and when Colonel Sher Ali learned that a Cadillac was to be raffled off for charity at a Fort Myer horse show after dinner, he took his guests there, saying: "I am going to win it. Then I shall drive you home in style."

Uniformed nurses passed up and down the aisles, selling chances on the car, but Jeane paid little attention until she overheard someone behind her say: "If Mrs. Dixon is so psychic, why doesn't she win the Cadillac?"

Thus challenged, she concentrated with closed eyes while holding several of the books of chances in her hand. Mrs. M. O. A. Baig, wife of a Pakistan Embassy counselor, tried to rush her by jesting: "Don't be so fussy, Jeane. Just take one. They're all alike."

Jeane selected one from the sixth book, wrote her husband's name on the ticket, and replied placidly: "You won't need to buy any more tickets, because this one is the winner."

Amused, the Indian colonel taunted: "All right, Jeane, if that is the one that will win, will you sell me your present car at a bargain?" Jeane promised to sell it for exactly what she had paid, although it was then worth considerably more on the scarce used-car market. The following Saturday night a telephone caller reported that James L. Dixon had won the Cadillac on a 14,000 to 1 chance, but Jimmy thought that a friend was teasing him until photographers from a local newspaper arrived the next morning to take a picture of him receiving the keys. True to her word, Jeane then sold the other car to Colonel Sher Ali for her own purchase price, and when he resold it at the close of his American tour of duty he realized an eight-hundred-dollar profit.

Within a short time after the colonel's return to his homeland, which had by then been partitioned, he moved to Pakistan. He rose rapidly to the rank of general and later became the Pakistani ambassador to Yugoslavia. Jeane had foreseen it all.

The news of her accurate forecast of India's partition had meanwhile found its way into newspapers here and abroad. The Earl of Jellicoe called her on his next visit to the British Embassy in Washington and invited her to lunch. How, he wanted to know, could she possibly have foreseen the partition two years in advance, on that exact date? After all, he marveled, only two days before the event announcement had been made that the House of Commons would not consent to partition. Jeane matter-of-factly explained that while reading for the Indian colonel the date had been shown to her in her crystal ball. The numerals, she amplified, were as clear to her as the prices listed on their luncheon menu.

Shrugging off his astonishment, she said: "People of the Far East are much easier to read for than Westerners, because they don't throw barriers in my way and things come through more clearly. Asians have the ingrained ability to let themselves go, in psychic matters."

After partition, oriental diplomats began beating a track to Jeane's door whenever affairs of state brought them to America. Once she read for a gentleman who identified himself as the astrologer for Prime Minister Jawaharlal Nehru and his sister, Madame Pandit. He came laden with hand-carved ivory gifts, but Jeane refused them. She also read for Madame Pandit's sister, Madame Raja Hutheesing, who came to Washington with her economist husband. Pakistan's first ambassador to the United States after partition was M. A. H. Ispahani. He had been in Washington only a few weeks before he telephoned Jeane to request an appointment. She remembers that his principal question was: "What is going to happen to Kashmir? Who will get it?" She told him that the thorny problem of Kashmir would continue for many years, and that fighting and bloodshed would occur before it was eventually solved.

Curiously enough, when M. Asaf Ali arrived in Washington to take over his duties as India's ambassador he also asked about Kashmir. Studying her crystal ball, Jeane told him that Kashmir was a province over which his country would fight. It is now history that war did break out between Pakistan and India over Kashmir, with fighting continuing until the United Nations arranged a cease-fire on January 1, 1949. The province is still a bone of contention, however, and Jeane sees no peaceful settlement "for some time to come."

Ambassador Asaf Ali further asked Jeane to tell him about the eventual disposition of Hyderabad, and she replied that it would go to India. This prediction was fulfilled when the state was incorporated into India in September 1948.

A leading industrialist of Hyderabad named Mir Laik Ali had meanwhile consulted Jeane and was also anxious to know what would happen to his native state. She told him that it would go to India, but not before he himself had been named Prime Minister of Hyderabad. Scoffing at her naïveté about world affairs, he said Hyderabad had never had a Prime Minister and never would. Undismayed, Jeane insisted that he would hold such a position and that shortly thereafter he would be taken prisoner. "But you will be rescued," she assured him. "It looks like some kind of strange bird coming out of the sky to pick you up and carry you to safety."

Suddenly he looked serious and in subdued tones confessed that he himself had had a vision that he would be taken prisoner. "Why do you come to me," she asked curiously, "when you have the same talent and ability that I have to foresee the future? You are the only person for whom I have read who also can read a crystal ball."

Mir Laik Ali admitted that he could do so but had wished to reassure himself that he was right. It was the last time Jeane saw the industrialist from Hyderabad but not the last that she heard of him. The next year Mr. M. O. A. Baig, counselor of the Pakistan Embassy, relayed word to her that Mir Laik Ali had become the first and only Prime Minister to the Nizam of Hyderabad, that he was subsequently jailed when India incorporated the state, and was rescued via helicopter (Jeane's "strange bird") by Mr. Baig's own brother.

Musing about these "readings" for oriental dignitaries, Jeane says: "Far Easterners depend a great deal on the lines in people's hands, and of course they believe in astrology. The first thing they invariably ask me is for permission to look into my hands. When they see a great half-moon and tremendous star on the palm of my right hand, they do so much bowing and scraping that I am embarrassed. They say that perhaps once in a thousand years is a person born with such a palm. Many of them seem to revere me as a prophet, but that is nonsense. Of course I am not!"

CHAPTER
7

JEANE'S psychic attunement to her family has always been acute. Devoted to her parents, she had never spent a night away from home until she married at the age of twenty-one. Shortly after her honeymoon, while on a business trip with her husband to New York, a strange premonition seized her as they walked into their hotel. "Jimmy," she said, clutching his arm for support, "we're going to have a tragedy in our family. Shall I call California?"

Patting the trembling hand on his sleeve, he soothed: "No, honey, it's just because you're away for the first time. You're probably homesick. If you'd like some music to cheer you up, I'll take you to Luchow's for dinner."

Accompanied by a friend of Jimmy's, they went to the famous German restaurant, but Jeane was too upset to touch her food. "A death is very near me," she insisted. "It's either my mother or my father." When the three returned to the hotel, a telegram was waiting. Jeane's mother, who had seemed perfectly well when they bade her good-bye earlier in the week, was dead. By telephone Jeane learned that her mother had accidentally struck her ankle against a chair. Apparently a leg infection suffered the previous year had not entirely cleared up, and she dropped dead of a blood clot that prevented circulation to her brain.

Another family tragedy occurred two years later, when Jeane and Jimmy were residing in Washington. Mr. Pinckert had begun to lose weight after his wife's death, and doctors diagnosed his disease as cancer of the throat. Little hope was offered for his recovery, but the urbane gentleman continued to live a reasonably normal life. One night Jeane awakened suddenly from an unusually deep sleep. "My father was standing beside my bed," she says, "just as he so often did in my childhood. I could hear his voice as clearly as you hear mine. He said that he had come to bid me good-bye. He told me that I must go on . . . that sometimes I would seem very much alone . . . that I would have to work hard . . . but more tranquil days eventually lay ahead."

Jeane immediately placed a call to her home in California and said sadly to her sister, "It has happened, hasn't it?"

"Yes, Jeane," her sister replied tearfully, "we sent you a telegram twenty minutes ago. Father is gone."

It was wartime and airplane accommodations were almost impossible to secure, but by this time Jeane had already begun to make a name for herself in Washington, and when a friend learned of her difficulty in obtaining passage, she pulled a wire or two. By midmorning Jeane received a call from the White House. An aide to President Roosevelt told her that a passenger had been bumped from his seat on a plane to California and the space was reserved in Jeane's name.

Shortly after her return from her father's funeral, Jeane stopped in to see a friend of hers. Supreme Court Justice Frank Murphy was there for Sunday brunch with a visiting relative and his long-time secretary, Eleanor Bumgardner. The latter says: "Jeane had been there no more than a couple of minutes when she signaled me to go into the dressing room.

As soon as we were alone she said: 'Lady, that relative is driving the Justice half crazy.' I knew it was true, but I did not understand how she could have known. She had never met either of them before, and no strain was apparent while Jeane was there."

Lady and Jeane became devoted friends. Both were dedicated to helping the less fortunate; Jeane has helped to support an uncounted number of white and Negro families. Miss Bumgardner was also busy "adopting." Her first ward was a fragile Chinese girl who had been washed ashore in the combat zone of Guadalcanal during World War II. No one knew the child's identity or which shipwreck she might have survived, but the U. S. Marines named her Patsy Li, which in Chinese means "Plum Blossom."

After the war, Samuel F. Pryor, Jr., vice-president of Pan American Airways, arranged passage to America for Patsy, and Lady Bumgardner, who had served in the Philippines with Frank Murphy while he was governor general there, volunteered to be her American guardian. Lady reared Patsy in her own home for twelve years, until the pretty ward married a young Chinese named Joe Buck Lee. Changing her name from Li to Lee was much less of a coincidence, however, than the fact that shortly before Patsy Li came to America she was reunited in an oriental orphanage with her Chinese parents, who had given her up for dead. By some miracle of chance, the lost child's real name turned out to have been—Patsy Li.

Jeane took an immediate interest in Patsy. The day they met she touched her little fingertips, picked up the child's vibrations, and said: "She has a strong will of her own. She has musical talents which can be developed, but she will become either a nurse or a doctor." Any of Miss Bumgardner's friends can testify to the strong and determined will exhibited by the Chinese girl in the next dozen years; she did well in her music, and became a nurse.

One day, while lunching privately with Miss Bumgardner in Justice Murphy's Supreme Court office, Jeane abruptly said: "Lady, you're going to have a new position."

Miss Bumgardner firmly replied that she had no intention of working for anyone except Justice Murphy, who had been her boss since he was mayor of Detroit seventeen years before. "And you're going to buy a sweet little house. It looks as if it's in Georgetown," Jeane continued, as if she had not heard the interruption.

Slightly annoyed, Lady snapped: "I don't want a house; I want an apartment. I'm tired of living in a hotel room after all these years, but I certainly don't intend to take on the problems of a house."

Jeane continued to stare into space. "Someone very dear to you will pass away suddenly in a few days," she said. "He is an older man. You must prepare yourself for the shock."

Miss Bumgardner recalls that this bothered her enough to ask if it were her father. When Jeane replied that the man was not a relative, Lady flippantly brought the luncheon to a close by saying: "Sorry, Jeane, but you're wrong about everything." Looking back on that day, Miss Bumgardner marvels: "Within two weeks it all came to pass. I lost my chief. I was given the position of roving secretary to all nine justices. I bought a little house in Georgetown quite by chance."

One reason why the thought of Justice Murphy's possible death did not occur to her, when Jeane uttered those prophetic words, was that Lady knew he was planning to be secretly married the following week. The Justice had entrusted Lady with the wedding ring, and she and his fiancée, socialite Joan Cuddihy, intended to go to Michigan for the Catholic ceremony. Miss Bumgardner wondered afterward why she had been so dense about Jeane's prophecy, for when she confided to Jeane that her boss and Miss Cuddihy were about to be wed, Jeane had contradicted: "Oh no, they'll never be married."

With some asperity Lady retorted: "Oh yes, they will. I

have the ring in my purse, and I'm taking it to Michigan with me. Joan and I are going together."

The Supreme Court had adjourned for the summer, and Justice Murphy was vacationing in his home state of Michigan. A few days after the luncheon he was found dead of an occlusion, and Miss Bumgardner flew to Michigan for his funeral. On her return, the Supreme Court paid her the unusual compliment of making her a roving secretary for all the justices who needed extra help. That same week she stopped in to see her friend Louise Cromwell Heiberg, who had been the first wife of General Douglas MacArthur. Louise was selling real estate, and on seeing Lady she exclaimed: "I've just found a darling little house on O Street. It's exactly the kind you should have." Miss Bumgardner was not interested, but Mrs. Heiberg insisted on her seeing it, the lure proved irresistible, and she bought it immediately.

Miss Bumgardner says that she will never forget the first visit Jeane paid to her O Street house. "Other guests had already arrived, and we were sitting around in a circle talking; but as Jeane entered the living room a guest uttered a strange little shriek. We all looked toward her in surprise, and she apologized to Jeane, saying, 'For a moment I thought you were the Madonna.'"

It was not the first time that Jeane had had this odd effect on strangers. Shortly after the war a friend in her apartment building invited the Dixons and several others to a concert, and among the guests waiting in the apartment lobby was Mrs. Estelle Friedrichs, an assistant to David K. Niles at the White House. Mrs. Friedrichs, who had never before met the Dixons, relates: "As the elevator door opened I saw what looked to be the figure of an angel standing just inside. I was dumb-struck, until a beautiful woman wearing a flowing white chiffon gown and white fox cape stepped out. Her hair seemed to form a halo, and her face was like an angel looking at God. The shock of it is still with me."

Jimmy Dixon witnessed two other similar events. Shortly

after their marriage he and Jeane were strolling along Fifth Avenue, during a trip to New York, when two young women who had passed them suddenly wheeled, followed a few paces, and hesitantly touched Jeane on the shoulder. "Please excuse me," one of them said in awe-struck tones, "but you look just like the Madonna. Who are you?" Another time, in Detroit, Jimmy was giving a little newsboy a lift in the car when he stopped to pick up Jeane. "Gee, mister," the lad exclaimed, "she looks like an angel."

Lady Bumgardner, musing on these isolated incidents, says: "It is understandable. Jeane has the face and the look of an angel, there is such sweetness in her composure. An angel of mercy she surely is. No one will ever know all of the kindnesses that Jeane has performed for strangers and friends, because she never speaks of them. If I had not witnessed many of them I would have had no other way of knowing. I often go with Jeane on her jaunts, and her goal is nearly always to help someone in need. I have accompanied her to the Peace Plantation in Virginia where she is helping to support several families who had previously been on relief but are now learning to support themselves. I have gone with her to visit the sick and the dispirited. She has taken dozens of misfits, strays, and immigrants into her house and given them a new start in life."

A young woman whom I shall call Joan insists that Jeane saved her life. Although she does not wish her identity known, her eyes glow as she speaks of the gentle woman who revolutionized her thinking, gave her a job and renewed confidence in herself. She is a girl who had had everything, until suddenly in her teens her parents deprived her of all but the bare essentials. She was desperately unhappy and ran away from home several times. Jeane took her into her own home and gave her a job in an effort to help her find herself.

Joan volunteered the information that she was not really earning the money Jeane paid her. "I didn't believe in psychic things, and at first I thought that Jeane was a kook," she says. "For instance, one day she suddenly came over to my desk and said that I must stop wearing contact lenses or I would develop an eye infection. I just laughed at her. After all, I had been wearing them for several years without any difficulty, but two weeks later I developed abrasions and an eye infection. The doctor then found that my lenses were too tight." Joan eventually returned home, but conditions had not improved, and when she stopped in to see Jeane, she was dismayed by her appearance. "Mrs. Dixon, you look quite ill," she cried in alarm.

Jeane reached for her hand, saying: "Joan, I have just seen a vision of you locked behind bars. If you don't do as I say and stay at home nights, something terrible will happen to you which will not be entirely your own doing."

The teen-ager was not about to listen to such preachment from adults. She was miserably unhappy with her parents, and they were totally unsympathetic to her problems. A few days later she went to a party with an older crowd and stayed all night with one of the women. The next morning she asked to borrow her hostess' car to keep an appointment with the doctor, although she had no driver's license. As she was driving along the street her older brother happened to spot her and gave chase in his car, cutting sharply in front of her. To avoid hitting him she swerved and struck a detective. Almost before she knew it she was in a juvenile detention ward. The owner of the car, fearful that she would get in trouble for letting Joan drive without a license, claimed that it had been taken without her permission. Joan's parents failed to come to her defense, and when she refused to be turned over to their custody, the judge sent her to a mental institution for disturbed children. Jeane found her there, after Joan had tried to take her life with an overdose of sleeping pills. In her loving way, she pumped new faith into the girl and forecast that she would be released on a specific date.

"The day after the date that Mrs. Dixon had mentioned,"

Joan recalls, "a policeman knocked at my door and said that a special hearing had been arranged for my case. The new judge heard my story and said that I had no business being in a mental ward. He set me free."

Miss Bumgardner says: "Jeane studied Joan's vibrations and found that she could write poetry if she would try. This awakened a new interest in her life. After she was released from the mental hospital Jeane took her into her home again."

During various periods when Joan lived at the Dixons' she saw a side of Jeane that is unknown to most of her friends in the Washington social whirl. Joan says wonderingly: "After the servant went to bed, Jeane would stay up late into the night cooking nourishing soups for poor people who were ill. I would take the soup to them the next day. Each morning Jeane would squeeze carrot juice for several elderly shopkeepers along Connecticut Avenue, near the Dixon real estate office. I remember one old blind lady who had a flower shop, and Jeane faithfully took her fresh carrot juice every morning on the way to Mass.

"There was an eccentric old lady living not far from the Dixons, in a house without electricity. Jeane used to send me over with baskets of food and have me run errands for the woman. You must remember that I was doing all of this on time for which Jeane was paying me. Even more amazing to me was how much time Jeane personally gave to these pathetic people. Sometimes she would be out very late at night, if she had a call for help. When the elderly eccentric broke her leg, Jeane personally fed her, nursed her, and drove her back and forth to the doctor's office. But the old lady was proud and wanted to pay for whatever she could. She insisted upon buying two-day-old bread, for instance, because it was cheaper. Jeane had the faculty for understanding such pride, and she would send me clear across town to a bakery to purchase this stale bread with the woman's money,

even though it cost Jeane many times that an
time and carfare."

Although Joan was a Protestant, she occasio
panied Jeane to Mass at St. Matthew's, and one
had an unforgettable experience. "I had been
times before with Jeane," she says wonderingly, but on this
particular morning I happened to glance toward her while
she was praying, and she wasn't there. This may sound silly,
but the place beside me was absolutely vacant. All I could see
was a soft haze of light and the empty pew. In a moment, of
course, she was back, quietly praying as before. It was a pro-
found experience. I still don't believe in psychic things, but I
believe utterly in Jeane."

While Joan was living at the Dixons' she often took telephone calls when Jeane was out, from people who would say:
"Please tell Mrs. Dixon how much we appreciate the food she
sent," or "Tell Mrs. Dixon that we want to thank her for the
clothing." Jeane had not previously mentioned these favors
to Joan. "Jeane is not like anyone else I have ever known,"
Joan says reflectively. "She's not like those who do volunteer
work for the Junior League, or Red Cross, or other organized
groups and get a certain amount of recognition for it. She
never lets anyone know what she does. When I've tried to tell
her how grateful I am for all she's done for me, she just says:
'Joan, if a person helps someone else, and then that person
helps another, it sets up a chain reaction. All I ever ask of you
is that, if the opportunity arises and you are able, you will
help someone else in need. That's the only thanks I want."

Joan says of Jeane: "People think she's naïve because she's
so gentle and kind, but she's sharp as a tack. No one fools her.
From time to time she has cautioned me about my friends,
'Stay away from that one; her vibrations are bad,' or 'That
one is okay.' It's really eerie how she invariably turns out to
be right."

Although James Dixon is one of Washington's leading

realtors, who drives shrewd bargains for his clients, his heart is apparently as bottomless as Jeane's. Just as Hollywood director Hal Roach gave him his start in the business world, so Jimmy has given similar boosts to hundreds who were faltering and uncertain. Whenever Jeane has asked his permission to help support someone, or to take a lonely immigrant into their home, he has gladly assented. Of his wife, Jimmy says:

"One of Jeane's most remarkable traits is the guidance and assistance that she has given to teen-age girls who have strayed from the straight and narrow. During the twenty-five years of our marriage she has put her protective arm around at least a hundred youngsters in trouble—some of them pregnant and unmarried. She has rescued young girls off the street, secured the release of many from jails and detention homes, and assumed the responsibility for their future conduct. Many of these cases we kept in our own home. Jeane and I never discuss their situations with a living soul. When we leave the house of a morning, we never remember who has been there, in order to protect their privacy. We don't even discuss their problems between ourselves. We simply feel that it is our duty to assist our fellow men whenever and wherever we can do so."

Both are pushovers for lost or abandoned animals. They have trailed stray dogs and cats all evening in every kind of weather, and then taken them to a veterinarian hospital for baths and shots. Jeane nurses the sick ones and keeps them until she can find good homes for them.

"Perhaps I shouldn't tell this," Jimmy muses, "but Jeane is so loaded with kindness that she has been mentioned four times in the wills of people I barely know; just token remembrances—like an antique box or a picture—but something they treasured and wanted Jeane to have as a remembrance. Often it was all they had to leave."

One token was from an elderly crippled woman whom Jeane had noticed limping through the lobby of her apartment building. Hastening to her side, she took the woman's elbow and put her into a cab. From then on she did innumerable kindnesses for the old lady, and because of her graciousness she was mentioned in the woman's will.

Another time a stranger called to tell Jeane that an old man whom she had befriended had passed away and his funeral was to be held that afternoon. Although it was one of her busiest days, she hesitated only a moment before responding: "That poor, sweet man. He had so few friends left that we may be the only ones there. Of course I will come." She canceled several appointments to attend the funeral, and only four other mourners were there. A few weeks later a banker called to tell her that the old man she thought was penniless had left her several thousand dollars. She spent the money on others.

CHAPTER
8

In the crowded hallway of an embassy Jeane shook hands with a stunning blonde to whom she had just been introduced. "Ah, you are of the nobility," Jeane said, smiling. There was nothing in the name or dress to give that fact away. The meeting took place at a charity tea. Neither had heard of the other, yet Mrs. Kitty Denny was born the Baroness Von Ammon; her great-grandfather had been Baron Christopher Frederic Von Ammon, a nineteenth-century Prime Minister of Saxony; her father, Baron Franklin Von Ammon, who practiced law in Pittsburgh, dropped the title.

Intrigued by the slim, angelic-looking woman with the straightforward approach, Kitty cornered Jeane and poured out her heart. She was in the process of getting a divorce, she confided, and deeply in love with a young navy commander. "We're going to be married just as soon as my divorce decree becomes final," Kitty rhapsodized.

Instead of beaming her approval, Jeane touched her fingertips and said: "This man will never marry you."

Irritated by what she thought was a curt remark, Kitty

retorted: "You are wrong, Mrs. Dixon, because nothing on earth will prevent me from marrying him—or him me. We are in love."

Jeane unobtrusively touched her fingertips again and continued as if there had been no interruption: "This man will go out of your life as suddenly as he came into it. You might as well prepare yourself."

Kitty recalls that when she subsequently told her fiancé about Jeane's prophecy he snapped: "She may be your friend, but she'll never be mine. I don't wish to meet her." Three weeks later newspapers headlined the crash of a navy plane in the Potomac River. Three of the seven passengers were saved, and the bodies of three others were quickly recovered. Kitty's fiancé was missing, and divers vainly sought the body. Jeane kept the lonely vigil with Kitty and counseled: "There is a coffin for him. I see it in the crystal ball. His body will be found." Several days later a fisherman pulled the lifeless body ashore. The grief-stricken Mrs. Denny paid little attention as Jeane said soothingly: "Kitty, there is a wonderful man coming into your life in about two years, who will bring you the greatest happiness and fulfillment that you have ever known. His front teeth are set wide apart, and he has red hair."

The inconsolable young woman said she knew of no one by that description and would not be interested if she did. He sounded "ugly," and she liked handsome men. Ignoring her protests, Jeane continued: "He isn't even in this country now, but you will meet him. If you had married the commander you'd have wanted to divorce him for this man when you ultimately met him."

At loose ends, Kitty took a job in the Dixon office. One day in 1946 Jeane sent her to accept a listing on a house which an army major, who had just returned from Alaska, was putting up for sale. When Kitty rang the doorbell of the impressive house in northwest Washington a redheaded major answered her ring. He smiled, and she noticed that his front teeth were widespread.

Major George Racey Jordan told her that he was selling the house because his divorce was pending and he was moving to the West Coast. She realized, of course, that he fitted Jeane's description, but she says of that meeting: "It was certainly not love at first sight. George began taking me out to dinner, and our casual friendship gradually ripened into the deepest love that I have ever known. We were married less than two years later, on November 5, 1948. Just as Jeane foretold, George is the finest man I've ever known."

By a previous marriage, Kitty Jordan had two beautiful daughters. Before Kitty Junior married, Jeane told her mother that it would end in divorce and that the girl would marry again. This has already come to pass, as has the prophecy that she made about the other daughter, Nancy Rogers. Kitty Von Ammon Jordan will never forget the morning that Jeane warned her to get Nancy out of Washington immediately. The beautiful titian-haired young girl had just returned to the capital, leaving her husband, Robert Dean Rogers, on a ranch near Seattle, Washington. He had been drinking heavily, and they had not been getting along, so Nancy had left him and was now living in an apartment by herself.

"Jeane told me that unless Nancy left Washington right away a terrible tragedy would occur," Kitty told me with a break in her voice. "She said Nancy would either kill herself or be murdered." Because she believed in Jeane's precognitive powers, Kitty urged her daughter to give up the new apartment and leave town. Nancy, who was thoroughly enjoying the social whirl with old friends, retorted that she had "handled Bob before" and could do so again.

Major Jordan, author of the postwar best seller, *Major Jordan's Diary*, was much in demand on the lecture platform, and his wife usually accompanied him on out-of-town trips.

They were staying at the Waldorf-Astoria in New York, where Jordan was to speak that evening, when the tragic news reached them that, three weeks after Jeane's somber forecast, Nancy was dead. Rogers, they learned, had traced his estranged wife to the apartment Jeane had wanted Nancy to vacate. Failing to talk his wife into a reconciliation, he shot her three times and then turned the gun on himself. It was both murder and suicide.

Discussing the tragedy, during a recent visit to Washington from her present home in Bel Air, California, Mrs. Jordan said: "It was all so unnecessary, but how can you force a married daughter to leave town, unless she is willing to go?" Kitty Jordan was also deeply attached to her mother, whose second husband was Edwin Wright Robinson, a prominent Pennsylvania manufacturer of mining cars. In talking with Kitty one day in the summer of 1953, Jeane had told her: "Within a year your dear mother will leave us, so you must prepare yourself to go on without her. She will die of cancer. I get a figure 9 around her very clearly, but I don't know the significance of it." Mrs. Robinson seemed in excellent health at that time, but on May 1, 1954, she died of cancer at Adrian Hospital in Punxsutawney, Pennsylvania. Her hospital room was Number 9.

Of Jeane, Kitty Jordan says: "If ever there was an angel on this earth, she is it. Jeane has never had an unkind thought. Her whole spirit is attuned to helping others. If only they would listen to what she tells them, so much misery could be avoided!"

In Europe I talked with an extremely wealthy woman who acknowledges her deep indebtedness to Jeane Dixon. They first met at a luncheon at the Mayflower Hotel in Washington. Betty had been planning to return to New York that afternoon, but Jeane warned: "Please drive very slowly and carefully, or a bad accident will occur." Betty said she was superstitious enough to heed the warning. Instead of racing along at her usual clip on the open highway, she was hugging the right lane in slow traffic, when without warning the gas line in her car suddenly broke in two. She was able to pull onto the shoulder of the road without mishap, but in the high-speed center lane, she believes, her car would have gone out of control and been struck from behind.

The next time Betty came to Washington she took Jeane to lunch and confided that she had decided to leave her husband. Jeane, touching her fingertips, told her that she must not do so. "He needs you very much, Betty," she cautioned. "If you go back to him with love in your heart you'll be living in a completely different world within six months, and will forever after be glad that you remained with him." It was not the advice that Betty wanted to hear. She nevertheless listened carefully while Jeane accurately described a sister of her husband's saying: "She also needs you. You think she doesn't like you, but she does, and you must pour out your love to her. You'll never regret it."

Two days before the six months elapsed, Betty telephoned Jeane from Union Station in Washington, saying that she had to see her at once. Jeane, busy with real estate appointments, hesitated, but the urgency in Betty's voice was strangely compelling. She therefore agreed to meet her friend in a restaurant. Betty, dressed in black, embraced her and said: "Jeane, I could never have forgiven myself if I had not gone back to Howard. We've had six happy months together. He died yesterday, and I'm taking him home for burial, on the train." Betty had also made a valiant effort to be kind to her sister-in-law, who lived only a short time longer. When the two wills were probated, her husband and his sister had left Betty over ten million dollars.

Commenting on her correct forecast, Jeane said: "If Betty had not gone back with love in her heart, which she did, it would not have turned out this way. That is why I didn't tell her that I foresaw both deaths. I did not want her to think of them in a mercenary way, and she didn't."

A year later Betty telephoned Jeane from New York to ask whether she should buy "the most beautiful necklace that I have ever seen." The price was a hundred and twenty-five thousand dollars. Instead of replying directly, Jeane cautioned: "Betty, if you look out of your window you'll see a man loitering across the street. He is watching to see if you are at home. He wants to blackmail you and will be ringing your doorbell shortly. Whatever you do, don't answer the door personally. Tell your maid to get his name and phone number, and turn it over to your lawyer."

Although Jeane was speaking from Washington, Betty looked out of her New York window and saw a young man whom she vaguely recognized. As she watched, he started toward her apartment lobby. She had a few minutes to instruct the maid, before he rang the doorbell. His name and telephone number were subsequently referred to Betty's lawyer, who contacted him and reported that the young man she had once befriended was now trying to blackmail her with some letters she had written. He wanted to get married and was desperate for funds. Betty reported this to Jeane and asked again: "But what about the beautiful necklace?" Jeane laughingly told her that she would get it, but that if she waited a few more weeks the price would be drastically reduced. A month later Betty acquired it for sixty-five thousand dollars.

CHAPTER
9

ON a humid midsummer evening in 1947 a management consultant named Daniel Magner dropped in at the Dixons' to talk over with his friend Jimmy his forthcoming trip to the Far East. The drone of an electric fan provided a sleepy accompaniment as he described his itinerary in minute detail. Jeane, seated across the room, was following his account with somnolent detachment, but just as he mentioned New Delhi a vision appeared before her, and she blurted: "Mahatma Gandhi will be assassinated."

The two men turned to stare at her. "What are you saying, Jeane?" Magner asked.

"It's true," she replied, her voice tinged with excitement. "Just as you spoke of India I saw a vision of the Prime Minister, and he was lifting up his arms to a religion that is too pro-Western for some of his people to tolerate. He was actually reaching toward God in the Christian sense. He'll be killed within six months by someone they least suspect." Within six months, on January 3, 1948, the great spiritual leader of India met an untimely death. His assassin was a Hindu fanatic who belonged to the Mahasabba politico-religious group.

By this time, Jeane's forecasts had been appearing frequently in newspapers, and people were besieging her for private readings. She could no longer go to parties without being backed into corners by people who held out their palms and pleaded for guidance about personal decisions. Her telephone rang at all hours of the night and Jimmy was losing sleep. One evening when a military attaché of a Far Eastern embassy knocked on their door to seek a reading, Jimmy Dixon decided that he had had enough. Politely but firmly he told the caller that Mrs. Dixon had retired for the night and could not be disturbed. Then he had a serious talk with his beautiful young wife.

"Charity begins at home, Jeane," he told her. "These people are imposing on your good nature and sapping your strength. Since you seem to find it impossible to refuse them, I think you'd better come to work in my office. The switchboard operator can help to protect your privacy, and you'll have a legitimate excuse when people want to take up your time."

Jeane conceded the logic of his plan, for she knew the constant readings drained her of needed energy. Therefore she accompanied Jimmy to his office the next morning and accepted the desk assigned to her. She even forced a smile when he told the apartment maid and the office receptionist: "I don't care who calls Mrs. Dixon, whether it's a king or an ambassador; just tell them that she can't be disturbed."

The pressure lessened somewhat after that, and she plunged zestfully into the business of bringing the right people and the right houses together in happy merger. She made no attempt to utilize her crystal ball to help with realty deals, but she could not still her psychic powers entirely. Victor Rand, a longtime employe, recalls that Mrs. Dixon telephoned him early one morning and said: "Mr. Rand, I dreamed that we had a fire in one of our houses. You'd better go over and check." Inwardly thinking "what next?" he dutifully stopped on his way to work by the vacant house she had mentioned. The moment he turned the key in the lock and pushed open the door he smelled smoke.

"I rushed to throw the light switch and call the fire department," he says. "Since then, if she tells me that there's trouble somewhere, or that we'll have difficulty with a certain deal, I cringe. I know we will have, because she's invariably right."

By 1948 Jeane had become interested enough in houses to want one of her own. After six years in Washington apartment life had begun to pall, and when the Dixons bought a house in exclusive Chevy Chase, just off Connecticut Avenue, Jeane discovered that she was a frustrated interior decorator at heart. She was having a delightful time "doing over" the house to meet her exacting specifications, when Jimmy received a telephone call from Mr. Stanley Posner, who asked how much he wanted for the Chevy Chase house. Mr. Dixon explained why it was not for sale, but the caller would not take "no" for an answer. "Just name your price," he insisted. "I want that house." To Jeane's consternation, Jimmy sold it.

The house hunting began again, finally narrowing down to two town houses: one on Sheridan Circle in the heart of Embassy Row, which Jimmy wanted; the other a slightly less pretentious house on Nineteenth Street, nearer the office, of which Jeane rhapsodizes: "The moment that I walked into that Nineteenth Street house I seemed to feel God putting his arms around me. I knew it was for me. All the vibrations were right."

Jimmy vehemently argued against it. For one thing it was grossly overpriced, as Jeane admitted, and when she signed the purchase papers anyway, he irately warned that he would not live in it. For the first time in their married life Jeane had dared to cross her husband, but she serenely set to work restoring and redecorating the four-story Victorian row house. Three weeks before its completion Jimmy dropped by to take a grudging look and finally asked: "When are we moving in?"

With a saucy tilt to her chin, she replied: "But I thought you weren't going to."

"Well, it's close to the office," he conceded. They have been living happily ever after in Jeane's dream house, and Jimmy, who adores his wife, never misses a quaint custom that he began during their honeymoon. Each night he places a fresh sweetheart rose on her pillow; or if he is out of town he has a rose delivered to her daily. "Like most husbands, I suppose that I don't say 'I love you' as often as I should," he explains, "so I substitute the little sweetheart rose in case I fail to do so."

Shortly after moving day they dined at the home of Dr. Stephen F. Verges and his wife, Evelyn, and Mrs. Verges persuaded Jeane to bring out the cards with which she sometimes "looks into the future." No sooner had Evelyn cut the pack than Jeane exclaimed: "Evelyn, you're going to be quite ill, and the doctors won't be able to diagnose the cause. At times you'll be sure that you are dying, but you'll get well, so hold onto that thought when it happens. The illness comes and goes in waves like a tide. I want to prepare you, so that you won't be frightened. Just accept this, and hold onto your faith." A short time later Evelyn Verges became desperately ill. Since her husband was a physician she had the best available medical care, but despite frequent medical consultations her condition worsened.

"No one could diagnose my trouble," Mrs. Verges says with a shudder. "I would be up for a day or two; then bedridden for ten. There was talk of brain tumor, blindness, and other dreadful things, but gradually I became stronger. Some time later I became pregnant, and the first month went well. Then I became very ill and despite numerous medical consultations grew steadily worse. In desperation I telephoned

Jeane and begged her to tell me the truth. I was afraid I was dying."

Jeane meditated before replying, and then told Evelyn that she could never have the child, or it would take her life as well as its own. This was devastating news to Evelyn, who had two children already and hoped for six, so she decided to endure the sickness and try to bear the baby. "I was completely bedridden and could take no food," she recalls. "All the top specialists had been called in on my case, but I was becoming too weak to care whether I lived or died. One morning my husband was shaving, when he heard the death rattle in my throat. He rushed to a chest of drawers, grabbed a bottle of Pedro Domecq brandy which the Spanish ambassador had sent, and poured most of it down my throat. I felt myself slipping and floating away. My husband frantically located a famous gynecologist who rushed me to the hospital and operated immediately to take the foetus which was costing my life. Just as Jeane had foreseen, the operation revealed that the child would have had no chance for survival anyway."

Mrs. Verges was present when a beautiful young woman showed Jeane a photograph of her fiancé. On touching the picture, Jeane told the girl that this was not the man she should marry and strongly urged her to wait until the right one came along. But the marriage occurred almost immediately, and by the time a baby had been born a year later, the young woman realized her dire mistake in not listening to Jeane.

"It was a living nightmare," Mrs. Verges says. "The details are too unspeakable to relate, but she had to flee to save her life. If only she had heeded Jeane's clear warning! But who can tell a young girl in love to pull in the reins and turn away from danger? Jeane feels that we have to meet these dangers in order to grow through them and test our faith. Thank God she uses His gift to help, to guide, to give courage and sup-

port. She has no malice in her heart towar
those who have deliberately hurt her. She is a
woman who feels that God has tests for eac
courage, love, faith, and endurance."

Evelyn Verges bears witness to another
phetic utterances, which occurred as the two women we
flying together to New York in the late fall of 1961. Express-
ing concern about someone close to both of them, Mrs.
Verges confided that the woman had threatened to commit
suicide. As she said the word "suicide," Jeane had a psychic
flash and murmured: "No, she never will; but Marilyn Monroe will."

"Marilyn Monroe!" Evelyn exclaimed. "Why, Jeane, what
makes you say such a thing about that adorable young woman
who has everything in the world to live for?"

"I know," she said, "but it will happen within the next
year. I have just seen it." Evelyn Verges was in Italy nine
months later when newspapers headlined the shocking news
that the beautiful blonde movie star who had sung "Happy
Birthday" greetings at President Kennedy's party in New
York a short time before had taken her life with sleeping
pills.

Marilyn Monroe's is not the only tragic death of strangers,
who were merely names in the news to Jeane, that she has
foreseen. Eleanor Bumgardner recalls that while discussing
plans for a trip abroad in the late summer of 1961, Jeane
abruptly exclaimed: "It's all right, Lady, so long as you don't
fly in the same plane with Dag Hammarskjold in mid-Septem-
ber. His plane will crash and he'll be killed." Lady, who had
never met the Secretary-General of the United Nations, dryly
remarked that they had no mutual travel plans. She was in
Europe on September 18 when she read that Hammarskjold
had died in a plane crash in Northern Rhodesia, while on a
mission seeking to establish a cease-fire between UN and
Katanga forces in the Congo. Jeane was right again, but how

es she do it? She says only: "I saw it happening while I was talking to Lady. It would have done no good to try to warn Mr. Hammarskjold. He knew nothing about me and would have paid no attention."

Many of Jeane's premonitions are less dramatic but equally amazing to friends whose lives they touch. Emma Perley Lincoln, a former newspaper writer who moderated a Washington radio program during and after World War II, recalls that she first met Jeane at a charity benefit party at the Sulgrave Club in 1944. Jeane was giving readings with her crystal ball to aid the Red Cross and the waiting line was long, but when the chair beside Jeane at last was vacant, "Bab" Lincoln slipped into it. She was worried about another person, and therefore asked: "What will happen to a close friend of mine named Alice?"

Jeane studied her crystal ball before replying: "Your friend has been separated from her husband for a long time, but she'll go back to him within two or three months."

Bab says of the incident: "Alice and her husband had been divorced for nearly fifteen years and the idea of their going back together was so ridiculous that I had to laugh. I knew the case intimately, and I knew that she had not seen him for several years, because he was an alcoholic." Within a month after the party, however, Alice had a telephone call from her former husband, who reported that he had been rehabilitated through Alcoholics Anonymous and wanted to see her again. A month later they were remarried.

Miss Lincoln was so impressed by Jeane's psychic power that she persuaded her to read for her sister in the spring of 1952. Jeane told Mrs. Dorothy Hawley that she saw "two lovely little grandchildren." When Mrs. Hawley replied that she had only one, Jeane smiled conspiratorially: "Then your daughter hasn't told you that she's pregnant again, because she is." Her daughter lived in another city, but Dorothy immediately telephoned her to ask if she were pregnant. The young woman was astonished. "How did [ ] Mother? I only just found out myself."

Jeane was reading publicly at a charity fu[ ] 1953 when she saw a vision of the Supreme [ ] above the seal of the Chief Justice a chair d[ ] "Oh dear," she wailed, "the Chief Justice wi[ ] few months." Those who heard her told their friends, and when Chief Justice Fred Vinson died unexpectedly in September, newscaster Hazel Markel related the curious story of Jeane's prophecy on her national radio program.

my—God Mother

Jeane is in constant demand for radio and television interviews, and Mrs. Shirley Peick recalls that once when she accompanied Jeane to a TV studio a disbelieving cameraman teased her rather unmercifully. "Mrs. Dixon had never seen him before, but as usual she was patience personified," Mrs. Peick says. "She made no attempt to defend herself or to argue with the man. Instead, she told him that she saw a brand-new baby near him. The man was astounded. With a decided change of attitude he said that his wife had given birth to a little girl the night before."

Helen Rouse, wife of the vice-president of a Washington savings and loan association, is another who can attest to Jeane's strange powers of precognition. When she first met Jeane in 1949 she was working for a cosmetics firm, and in the process of getting a divorce. Sensing her depressed mood, Jeane touched her fingers and said: "Don't be disturbed. Within two years you will marry a perfectly wonderful man who is just right for you. He has blue eyes and light, prematurely graying hair. I see that his initials are G.R. You will be happier and more prosperous than ever before." The future Mrs. Rouse must have reflected her disbelief, for Jeane added: "You already know him. You have known him since you were a teen-ager."

friend who came to see me in Columbia Hospital

Helen vainly racked her brain for anyone she had known with the initials G.R., and finally put the prediction out of her mind. Shortly after her divorce she entered a savings and

ุ1 company to open an account and was hailed by Pete
ศouse from his desk. She had scarcely seen him since they
were classmates at Central High School, but he told her:
"You'll be surprised to hear that I'm getting a divorce."
Helen mentioned her own recent divorce, and after his decree became final Pete invited her to dinner. A six-month
courtship ensued, during which Helen learned for the first
time that Pete was only a nickname; he had been christened
Gordon Rouse. Not only had Jeane foreseen the correct initials, but the remainder of the description also fitted, and
Helen has been happily married to the "perfectly wonderful"
blue-eyed man for fourteen years.

Mary Goldsmith, an executive at the International Team-
sters' Union headquarters in Washington, was one of those to
whom Jeane foretold President Kennedy's assassination a
week before the tragic event. Mary had previously witnessed
other manifestations of Jeane's psychic talent, and she told
me about a business luncheon which the two of them had
with a policeman and a civilian who were active in a government rehabilitation project.

The men had never met Jeane before, but when Mary mentioned her seeming ability to foresee the future, the elderly
policeman joshingly asked what he had in store. Instead of
dipping into the future, Jeane told him: "When you were
fifty something happened to you that changed all the rest of
your life for the better." Touching the younger man's hand,
she said: "You're about thirty-seven. When you were sixteen
something tragic happened to you which changed your life
for the worse."

Jeane left shortly for another appointment, and the two
men turned to Mrs. Goldsmith in astonishment. The policeman spoke first, saying: "I was an alcoholic until I was fifty
years old. Then I stopped drinking, and because I had been
rehabilitated through the help of friends, I determined to
dedicate my life to helping others."

The younger man cleared his throat and also decided to

confess, saying: "She said I was about thirty-seven, and I'm thirty-eight. I grew up in a very poor but strict Catholic family. My father was an alcoholic, and when he was drunk he would beat my mother. Finally, when I was sixteen I beat him up. It was the first time I ever laid a hand on him, but I ran away from home that night and joined the army. I was so shocked at what I had done that I started drinking and soon became an alcoholic. I finally married, but I was the kind of father that my own children ran from. At last I was cured by Alcoholics Anonymous, and that's why I'm in rehabilitation work now."

Mary Goldsmith recalled that another time, after accompanying Jeane to a radio station in Virginia, she and Jeane went to dinner with a physician unknown to Jeane. The conversation turned to the radio interview, and Jeane asked the doctor if she could look at his hands. He thrust them out, palms up, and Jeane lightly touched his fingertips. "When you were thirty-five some terrible tragedy occurred that changed the pattern of your life. It had to do with your wife."

Mrs. Goldsmith noticed that the doctor was unusually reserved during the remainder of the meal. Knowing his scientific turn of mind, she thought that he might be annoyed with the conversation, but after paying the check he cornered Mary in the foyer. "Listen," he said, "only three people in this whole world know what happened to me when I was thirty-five. My wife had a mental breakdown. We gave her shock treatment and did everything that the medical profession could offer, but it was hopeless. She had to be institutionalized, and our children sent away to live with relatives. Even they don't know about their mother. I can assure you that it drastically changed the pattern of my life. This friend of yours must have a rare gift from God."

Mary Goldsmith herself believed that Jeane's was a divine gift. She said that four years previously she had been troubled by severe abdominal pain and went into George Washington hospital for an examination. "Jeane told me that they would find something but not to worry, because it would not be cancer," Mary continued. "Extensive tests turned up nothing. I was hospitalized for nine days, but each test was negative. On a Friday, Jeane said they would find the trouble the following Tuesday morning. That Tuesday the doctors told me they had finally located an inoperable hernia in the chest cavity, which was pressing on my heart. They gave me treatments for it and sent me home."

When I talked to Mrs. Goldsmith in early 1964 she was in the hospital again. Before she checked in, Jeane sadly confided to John Teeter, of the Damon Runyon Cancer Fund: "This time Mary's illness is fatal. They will find cancer, and she has but a few months to live." Jeane's psychic diagnosis was speedily confirmed by medical tests, and in mid-July Mary died of cancer.

One of the more remarkable aspects of Jeane's strange talent is her seeming ability to glimpse yesterday or tomorrow with equal ease. When she reads for a person, the movie of his life apparently runs both backward and forward through her projector. Because of this faculty she was already becoming a household name in social and official Washington when she announced in January 1948 that President Harry S Truman would be re-elected that November. So few others thought so that Jeane's friends began to think she was losing her touch.

Mrs. Walter Maloney, wife of a Washington attorney, recalls that while Jeane was reading for her that January she told her to make a wish. Then Jeane studied her crystal ball and said: "Your wish is not a particularly personal one, but you're going to get it. It will come true." Feeling that she had tricked her friend, Mrs. Maloney laughingly confessed that she had wished for Mr. Truman's re-election, and the odds were heavily against it. Jeane told her that the wish would nevertheless come true, because she had seen his victory in the crystal ball. During this same period she telephoned her friend Estelle Friedrichs and told her not to worry about her job at the White House, because "Mr. Truman will be elected."

Her prediction spread rapidly through official circles, and some Washington hostesses irately crossed her from their party lists. A social secretary for one of the embassies even telephoned to urge that Jeane publicly change her forecast, "because you're making yourself ridiculous with this one." Jeane stuck by her guns. A few weeks later, appearing on Bab Lincoln's local radio program, Jeane forecast that the rival nominees would be Thomas E. Dewey and Harry S Truman. "I see Mr. Dewey disappearing in a flood of newspapers," Jeane said, "and a laurel wreath of victory descending over Mr. Truman's head." Political commentator Ray Henle also aired her prediction on his national radio program "Three Star Extra," and letters of abuse poured in on Jeane from all parts of the country. No one seemed to believe her, not even her friend Mrs. Friedrichs.

The Saturday before election Mrs. Maloney was working as a volunteer at Truman headquarters, soliciting donations in a last-ditch effort to buy broadcast time for the President's political speeches. Only a day or two before he had been cut off the air for lack of funds. Jeane stopped by to leave a contribution and complained: "Madeline, everyone thinks I'm crazy. Let's try it again with the cards, to see if I still get the same vibrations."

Thinking back to that busy day, Mrs. Maloney still smiles. "She brought out those worn old cards that she sometimes uses, and had me cut them. Then she spread them out. She didn't say anything for a few minutes, but she finally looked up and said she just couldn't see it any other way. Truman was going to win." And win he did, to the surprise of practically everyone but the President and Jeane. Four years later, during the 1952 campaign, Jeane told Mrs. Maloney that she saw a dark cloud over Adlai Stevenson. "He is not going to win," she said, "but his star is ascending, and someday he will take his rightful place in government. He will never, however, call the White House home. The Republicans will be in for two terms, and then the Democrats for two terms." An ardent Democrat, Mrs. Maloney was naturally disappointed at this forecast. She remembers that Jeane continued: "I have seen Mr. Stevenson in a vision, and he's going to be very sick. He will be rushed to the hospital for an operation, but he will recover." She was soon to be proved right about this too.

Shortly before the nominating conventions that summer of 1952, television moderator Martha Rountree gave a large party in her Washington garden. Most of the potential candidates were invited, and Jeane was asked to bring her crystal ball. Reading for Averell Harriman and Senator Richard Russell, Jeane told them that they would be denied the Democratic nomination, and that the nominee's name would begin with an *s*.

Speaker Sam Rayburn posed for a picture with Jeane, who was dressed as a gypsy princess, and appeared visibly upset when she told him that he would lose the Speakership. "But you will be without your exalted position only for a short while," she reassured. "Then you will get your gavel back, and on your seventy-third birthday you will have the greatest honor of your entire career." The rest is history. Adlai Stevenson, whose name begins with *s*, won the nomination, but Republicans, riding the crest of the Eisenhower wave, recaptured control of the House and Senate that fall. GOP Representative Joseph W. Martin, Jr., supplanted "Mr. Sam" as Speaker of the House; but two years later the tide turned and he regained the Speakership. On his seventy-third birthday the Democrats staged a tremendous "Sam Rayburn dinner" which overflowed the hall, and President Eisenhower honored him with a plaque.

The next day Mr. Rayburn gallantly telephoned Jeane to say: "My belief in you is very great. The dinner was the greatest honor ever paid to me. You keep on doing the work that you're doing for people, because that prediction buoyed me up when things looked dark."

I first met Jeane the night of Martha Rountree's party, and subsequently wrote a column quoting her prediction that General Eisenhower would capture the White House. Jeane also told Hope Ridings Miller that the general would defeat Adlai Stevenson, and Hope was so disappointed that she asked to be notified immediately if the prediction changed. Mrs. Miller, now the editor of *Diplomat* magazine, recalls: "I was staying at the Waldorf in New York two weeks before the election, when I received a telegram from Jeane Dixon. She said it would be Eisenhower by a landslide. And it was."

The following spring, on May 14, 1953, Martha Rountree invited Jeane to appear with her crystal ball on an NBC television program. Before accepting, Jeane asked if it would be all right for her to talk about previous forecasts if she failed to see anything new in her crystal ball while on the program. Miss Rountree agreed, because Jeane solemnly pointed out that "you can't turn it off and on like a water spigot." Jeane also checked the date of the program astrologically, to establish that it was one of her "good" days. In doing so she used a system taught to her as a child in California by a Jesuit priest called Father Henry. By studying her own birth chart she had long ago determined that fives and nines were her best numbers, and that she should guard against fours and eights. May 14, 1953, therefore seemed like an excellent date. May is the fifth month, and since in numerology the numbers of a date are added together sideways, the one and four of the fourteenth day totaled five. By the same token, the year 1953 adds to eighteen, and eight and one make nine.

The show went on the air, and as former Ambassador to

Russia Joseph E. Davies stepped into camera range, Jeane was mentally rehearsing what she would reply about a recent vision concerning Nepal. Instead he asked: "How long will Malenkov be Prime Minister of Russia?" Everyone was uneasy except Jeane, who did not seem in the least perturbed at the prospect of fencing before television cameras with the famous Russian expert who had written the best-selling book, *Mission to Moscow*. Peering into her crystal ball, Jeane "saw" Malenkov being replaced by another man whose image was quite plain to her, and she replied, "He will bow out in slightly less than two years, to a man with an oval-shaped head, wavy gray hair, a little goatee, and greenish eyes."

The ambassador uttered a mirthless laugh. Displaying his superior knowledge of the Soviet Union, he retorted that Russian premiers are not peacefully replaced; they either die or are shot. Moreover, he added, Russians do not look like the replacement whom she described, so she was wrong on all counts. Jeane calmly replied that she was telling what she "saw," not what she "thought," and that the event would definitely transpire shortly before two years had elapsed, because she "saw a tiny tail on a two."

By now she had the complete attention of the group which included former Ambassador to China Patrick J. Hurley and his wife, Marine Commandant Lemuel C. Shepherd and Mrs. Shepherd, and Mrs. Davies, the former Marjorie Post, heiress to a cereal fortune. Jeane, however, seemed oblivious to everyone, because another picture was beginning to form in the crystal ball. Speaking out eagerly, she said that the goateed gentleman would rule only briefly, until a shorter, bald-headed man took over. "Shortly afterward," she continued, "a silver ball will go into outer space. It will circle the earth and come back to Russia, landing like a dove of peace on the bald head of the short, fat man. It will then dig its claws into his scalp." This meant, she explained, that after Russia launched the world's first orbiting object the Soviets would have enormous power. Jeane held out her hands in a circle to indicate the shape of the future sputnik.

At that point Ambassador Davies could contain himself no longer. Taking her by the arm, he rasped: "No, no, that will never happen. I have been ambassador there, and I know that things are not done that way in Russia."

Recalling the dramatic incident, Jeane sighs: "Much more was coming, but Mr. Davis actually grabbed my arm and shook me, saying that I should read his book and learn about Russia. I was so engrossed that I had forgotten we were on television. Otherwise I would not have said what I did next." Television viewers heard Jeane exclaim: "Oh, Mr. Ambassador, you've just spoiled my whole connection."

Mr. Davies was still poking fun at Jeane when the program ended, but he lived to see her proven right. One month short of two years later, Marshal Bulganin peacefully replaced Georgi Malenkov as the Soviet Premier. Gray-haired, goateed Bulganin fit Jeane's description precisely, and roly-poly, bald-headed Nikita Khrushchev took over the actual reins of power as the Communist party boss. In 1957 the Soviets orbited the world's first man-made satellite, and Khrushchev deposed Bulganin the following March. Back in 1953, however, Jeane's amused audience could not share her vision of the shape of things to come.

That same year John P. Philpott, an official of the American Federation of Labor's Retail Clerks Union, was at the Dixons' talking about a trip to California, when Jeane saw "a vision of a golden wedding ring" descending over his union and the Congress of Industrial Organizations.

"Oh, Mr. Philpott," she interrupted, "the AFL and CIO are going to merge."

"Never," he scoffed. "Never, never, never. They're worlds apart."

Unperturbed, Jeane insisted: "Nevertheless, they are going to merge, because I've seen a wedding for them. It will come within two years." On December 5, 1955, the CIO merged with the AFL.

Among the most closely guarded secrets of the Eisenhower Administration was the President's golf score. One May evening in 1953, Martha Rountree was helping stage a radio program for disabled veterans at Bethesda Naval Hospital in nearby Maryland, and had invited Jeane to participate in a segment of the show with comedian Bob Hope. I was appearing in another segment, as a panelist on Martha's TV program, "Leave It To the Girls," and was backstage when Bob Hope bustled in, to the cheers of the veterans. Jeane, wearing a long evening dress, was escorted on stage and introduced to Hope as Washington's famous seeress. The comedian cracked a few jokes and then teased: "Well, Mrs. Dixon, I've been playing golf with Ike this afternoon at Burning Tree. If you're so good, tell me what my golf score was."

Looking into her crystal ball, she replied serenely: "I'll tell you not only your score but also the President's. It was a 96 and a 92. You won."

The smile faded from his lips, and for a moment Bob seemed in danger of collapse. As soon as the show was over, he grabbed his manager-brother backstage and groaned: "Jack, this Dixon woman has ruined me. The President will never believe I didn't give out his golf score." He then ordered the golf score trimmed from the tape that would be broadcast nationally on his regular show. He dared not air the fact that Ike had shot a 96.

CHAPTER
10

ONE Sunday in November 1954 a group of friends met in the Dixon realty office to discuss an exhibition that artist Emma Ench had arranged in her Paterson, New Jersey, home to benefit the Damon Runyon Cancer Fund. Miss Ench was seated in a chair near the door, Jeane Dixon sat behind her husband's big desk, and Lorene Mason was perched on a corner of the desk between them. Estelle Friedrichs, known to her friends as Mike, and Shirley Peick completed the circle.

Miss Ench had brought with her a stack of eight-by-ten photographs of the display; each scene illustrated a nursery rhyme such as "The Old Woman Who Lived in a Shoe." One by one she passed them to Lorene, who exclaimed at their artistic quality and handed them to Jeane, who also remarked on their beauty, and sent them on around the circle. Lorene Mason recalls that the tenth picture showed a cross section of the display in Emma's recreation room, which she considered particularly attractive, but as she handed it to Jeane the seeress dropped it as if her fingers were burned and cried out in horror: "Oh, Emma, you're going to have a terrible fire unless you're very careful!" Those present have reconstructed the ensuing conversation in this vein:

Emma: "Oh, pooh, Jeane, don't try to use that as an excuse for not coming up to Paterson to see the exhibit. The fire marshal has already been there and approved the arrangement."

Jeane: "Emma, please! I can't warn you enough to have everything fireproofed."

Emma: "Don't worry, Jeane; everything is fine, I tell you."

Jeane: "Emma, Emma, be careful. You must have everything in that room fireproofed or there will be a terrible tragedy. I beg you!"

Emma: "Jeane, don't keep saying that. I tell you the fire marshal says everything is fine."

Jeane: "Emma, please, please listen to me."

The meeting broke up in some embarrassment, and Miss Ench left with Mrs. Friedrichs. To Miss Mason, who remained behind, Jeane murmured in a tone of resignation: "Poor, poor Emma! Poor Emma!" The exhibit was scheduled to close on January 15, and two days later Jeane and Miss Mason flew to New York on Runyon fund business. As they walked into the office of the director Mr. Teeter's secretary exclaimed: "Isn't it ghastly about Miss Ench?"

She handed them a copy of the Paterson *Morning Call* dated January 17, 1955, whose eight-column banner headline read: PARTY FIRE KILLS MISS ENCH. The news story itself began: "The originator of a fairyland display for the benefit of the Damon Runyon Cancer Fund died last night in the Paterson General Hospital of burns she sustained in a fire which gutted the cellar where the display was located. Six other persons were burned, one seriously. Dead is Miss Emma Ench, 40, who had dedicated the display to her mother who had died of cancer.

"The fairyland dolls and houses, located on a large table in the cellar of the home of Richard Ench, had attracted hundreds of visitors since it was set up about a week before Christmas. Men, women and children who had been enjoying a party around the display were forced to flee up a flaming stairway at the back of the house. Firemen said a flaming marshmallow was responsible for the blaze.

"Witnesses said the marshmallow landed in the display called 'The Land of Let's Believe,' and within seconds flames spread through the dry evergreens and absorbent cotton, cutting off an exit through the garage."

The article went on to report that Miss Ench, after closing the exhibit, had decided to give a final party for the fifteen neighborhood children and adults who had helped her with the exhibit. She was worried about the dryness of the evergreens and had remarked that she must remove them the next day. The next day was too late. A child, toasting marshmallows in the fireplace, jerked the stick excitedly when the confection caught on fire, and it sailed into the powder-dry greens festooning the ceiling. Miss Ench, who was known in Paterson as "The Santa Claus Lady" because of her charitable endeavors each Christmastime, died after being dragged unconscious from the house.

Lorene Mason, gripping the newspaper which told of the catastrophe, stared dazedly at Jeane. "And you told her," she said. In retrospect it seems strange that Emma Ench should have so completely disregarded her friend's warning. She knew of Jeane's reputation as a psychic, and although she could not then know how accurate her predictions about Russia and the satellite were to prove, she did know about the Kentucky Derby of 1953. The year before the tragic fire, Jeane had received a telegram from racing friends in New York, asking whether they should bet on Native Dancer, the favorite in the Derby. Before replying to the wire, Jeane called Estelle Friedrichs and said: "I just don't see Native Dancer winning, but I don't see it losing, either. I'm confused." Mike replied that a horse does not have to come in first to be in the money, because it can also place or show. "That's it—place," Jeane ejaculated. "Dancer will come in second," and that is exactly what happened to the previously undefeated favorite.

Mrs. Friedrichs had had innumerable chances to observe her friend's uncanny powers. The Sunday morning following their first meeting she invited Jeane to stop by her apartment after Mass. When Jeane arrived Mike was wearing an expensive red silk polka-dot robe which she had purchased in New York the month previously after unexpectedly receiving an invitation to visit wealthy friends at their estate nearby. Jeane seated herself on the sofa but immediately began to shift uncomfortably, and finally ventured: "Do you have another robe you can put on? I just can't concentrate with that one around. It can bring you bad luck."

Although Mike herself considered the robe unusually becoming she good-naturedly retired to the dressing room and changed into another. When she reappeared, Jeane's voice reflected her relief. "Good," she said. "Just don't wear that other one any more. Give it away. It may not bring bad luck to someone else, but it will to you." What Mrs. Friedrichs could not then know was that bad luck was already brewing for her. Because of the weekend spent at the house party for which she had bought the robe, she was soon to become innocently involved in a probe of a money transaction to which her hosts were party. Mike had known nothing of the deal, but when a government investigation was launched she was embarrassingly scrutinized because of her White House position.

The years passed, and as Jeane had predicted Mike stayed on at the White House under the Truman as well as the Roosevelt Administration. In the late spring of 1951 her boss, David K. Niles, told her he was resigning because of ill-health. He suggested that during his convalescence from an

impending operation she go abroad for a couple of months as
a working member of an official conference. Mike relished
the idea but refrained from committing herself until she had
asked Jeane for advice. Jeane advised her to go, saying: "It
will be like a college education for you. You think you will
be gone only two months, but actually you'll be gone for
seven." Mike didn't think so, and neither did the White
House. She sailed August 8, 1951, as a secretary to the U.S.
delegation to a Radio Administrative Conference which was
to open August 15 in Geneva and close in October. The
conference, called to assign international radio wave lengths,
extended on into early December, after which Mike used two
weeks of her vacation to visit Rome, Milan, Venice, Florence,
and Paris.

As soon as she reached Paris she applied for the first available transportation home, but during the Christmas season
space was at a premium, and while awaiting government
orders to sail she performed secretarial work for Mrs. Eleanor
Roosevelt, who was a United Nations delegate there. At
Christmas Eve church services in Paris she ran into Paul Hoff-
man, who upon learning that she was temporarily stranded
drafted her to work for the Emergency Relief Administration. Mike remained with the agency until March 8, when
she received word that her husband was ill and hastily flew
home. It had been seven months to the day since she set
sail.

Mrs. Friedrichs' husband speedily recovered from pneumonia, and shortly afterward they entertained the owner of a
large New York hosiery mill and the Dixons for dinner. At
the stranger's urging Jeane touched his fingers and forecast
that he would soon be tempted to start another business in a
somewhat related field, but that he should not do so, because
it would fail. She also said: "You have two daughters. The
elder will shortly marry, but it will end in divorce. Later she
will marry again and be very happy." Within a few months

hy manufacturer launched a lingerie business,
ed. The second prophecy also came true, and the
now happily married for the second time.

Early in 1954 Mrs. Friedrichs introduced Jeane to an old
friend, Anne Nichols, author of the highly successful play,
Abie's Irish Rose. Miss Nichols was then writing another
play, but when Jeane touched her hand she picked up vibrations and announced: "Anne, you are hoping to revive a play
of yours on Broadway. You will do it, too, but it will not be
successful." Mike had not known that her friend was even
considering a revival, but that November she received a
summons to come to New York and help with the rehearsals
for *Abie's Irish Rose.* The play opened in December, flopped,
and closed three weeks later.

In reading for Miss Nichols and other strangers, Jeane almost invariably asks their birthday. "I do that for the rising
and setting signs," she explains, "because it helps in my meditation to see which direction they're going. I don't ask for
the minute of their birth, because I don't want to be influenced by what their horoscope charts would say. I just like to
know their rising and setting signs, so that I can pick up their
correct vibrations."

Jeane marks her own calendar for "good" and "bad" days a
year in advance, after working out her chart. "If the day, the
month, and the year add up to a four," she says, "then I have
to be very careful on that particular date, because it's like a
ship being launched upon the ocean. It could be a wonderful
ship, but there's always danger if it gets caught in a storm and
suffers severe battering. Our lives take the same kind of beating as a ship on the seas. People can feel this storm within
themselves, when they are being buffeted by the wrong signs,
even if they don't know why. On a day that adds to four, my
judgment may not be quite as good as on one that adds to
five, seven, or nine. Five is my guiding number. Seven is a
miracle number, and nine signifies the ending of things and
the beginning of a new cycle."

Mrs. Friedrichs recalls that after Jeane had ascertained Margaret Truman's birthday, she said of her: "She is to be admired for pursuing a career while living in the White House, but she will never make a name for herself as a singer. She will not marry while her father is the President. Later she will be rather choosy in selecting a husband, and will not accept him without the approval of her parents."

Margaret Truman is now married to Clifton Daniel, a newspaperman whom she did not meet until after the Trumans left the White House. Her mother and father heartily approved her choice of a mate.

By the mid-fifties Jeane Dixon's prowess as a political prognosticator was so well established that newspaper and radio commentators began telephoning her from all parts of the nation to ask how the 1956 campaign was shaping up in her crystal ball. She had yet to be wrong in forecasting a presidential winner. She was right about Herbert Hoover's election in 1928, when she was still in grammar school, and she accurately foretold Franklin Delano Roosevelt's four victories as well as his death. She had foreseen that Harry Truman would become President "through an act of God," and that he would be re-elected in 1948. She also forecast the return of the Republicans to power in 1952 under the banner of Dwight Eisenhower.

Back in 1945, she had even dared to tell Prime Minister Winston Churchill that he would be turned out of office by the British electorate. This prophecy coincided with the distinguished wartime leader's trip to Washington earlier that spring. Lord and Lady Halifax had invited Mrs. Dixon to a party in honor of their visiting Prime Minister, and though Jeane knew nothing of Britain's political situation, she "received vibrations" when she shook Mr. Churchill's hand in the receiving line and beseeched him: "Mr. Prime Minister, please don't call an early election or you'll be defeated."

The grand old man of British politics turned to stare at the brash young woman. Her clear hazel eyes levelly returned his gaze, and after a moment he grunted: "England will never let me down."

As if she had not heard, Jeane continued: "But never mind. You'll be back in power in a few more years."

Churchill nevertheless set the elections for June of that year, and the Labor party captured control of Parliament. Churchill was replaced by Prime Minister Attlee, and six years elapsed before the Tories won again. Then Mr. Churchill reassumed the Prime Minister's mantle, which he proudly wore until his voluntary retirement in 1955.

In 1962, Jeane made another prediction about the great statesman. She told Russell P. Riley that Sir Winston would die at the end of 1964. She missed by only 26 days.

After I met Jeane in 1952 I began writing occasional columns about her forecasts, which gradually developed into an annual New Year's tradition. The column that appeared under my by-line in the New York *Daily News* on December 31, 1955, began as follows: "While dozens of senators and governors are confidently scribbling their New Year's resolutions—to run for the presidency—Washington's favorite seeress has been quietly studying her crystal ball. If Jeane Dixon's latest predictions prove as amazingly accurate as those of the past, presidential hopefuls can put away their campaign buttons. Her stars have already decreed that Dwight D. Eisenhower will be re-elected."

In that same column she forecast that Governor Frank Lausche of Ohio would make an important advancement, either into the new Administration or to the Senate, and added: "Senator Estes Kefauver will fail in his dream of the presidency, but is likeliest winner of second-place nomination on the Democratic ticket." Those predictions were published in my column eleven months before President Eisenhower was re-elected, and seven months before Senator Kefauver lost the Democratic presidential nomination, but won second place on the ticket in a spirited race with Senator

John F. Kennedy. And Lausche did indeed win election to the Senate that November.

Senator Kefauver was well aware of Jeane's prediction concerning himself, before he narrowly won the vice-presidential nomination in the convention fight of 1956. In January of that year a friend had telephoned Estelle Friedrichs to offer her a job with the Kefauver for President Committee. Before accepting she consulted Jeane, who studied her crystal ball and advised: "Take the job; but Senator Kefauver is not going to be President despite all of his campaigning and handshaking. He will be the vice-presidential nominee. I can tell you right now that the ticket will be Stevenson and Kefauver."

Mrs. Friedrichs took the position, and later that spring gave a reception where Jeane met Senator Kefauver for the first time. At Mrs. Friedrichs' suggestion she read for the Tennessee presidential hopeful and told him that his timing was wrong for a White House try. "You should have waited to make your bid until 1960, when the Democrats will win," she chided. "You will be nominated as Vice-President this year, but your party will be defeated."

Several months later, after Adlai Stevenson had been nominated for the second time as the Democratic standard-bearer and the selection of his running mate was thrown open to the delegates, Kefauver, Jack Kennedy, and Hubert Humphrey launched a free-wheeling scramble for delegate support. Recalling Jeane's prophecy, a member of the Kefauver staff telephoned her long distance from Chicago to say that it looked as if Senator Kennedy would probably win the race. What did she foresee? Jeane meditated for a moment and replied that Kefauver would definitely get the vice-presidential nomination. He did, and his party lost.

When Jeane predicted in December 1955 that President Eisenhower would be re-elected the following November, Ike himself was not even sure that he would run again. He was still convalescing from a heart attack which Mrs. Dixon had previously foreseen. Two days before the attack a high official in the Administration telephoned Jeane to say that he had been invited to the summer White House in Denver but was undecided whether to go. "You must go immediately, without delay," she responded, "because if you don't it will be too late. The President is going to be taken seriously ill."

Jeane had already asked a White House adviser to warn the President to stay away from the golf course for a time, but as usual no one listened. Two days later, after playing thirty-six holes of golf in Denver's rarefied atmosphere, the President suffered a heart attack. When the official telephoned to break the news of Ike's illness, Jeane replied calmly: "It's all right. He will recover and be better than before."

In the column of predictions for 1956, Jeane also declared: "President Eisenhower will be somewhat less active during his second four years of the presidency. He will run the government as you would a big business, delegating his less important powers and enjoying the job much more than he ever has before. It will be the most non-partisan four years in recent history. I see no atomic warfare in the near future, and little danger from Russia. Our big trouble will come from Communist China, and the strange thing is that the Red Chinese will soon turn on Russia too. We should begin to treat Russia simply as a keen competitor, because we will need her on our side when Red China becomes a world threat in 1964. The Democrats will capture the White House in 1960."

One of the most uncanny forecasts Jeane Dixon has ever personally made to me came in December 1958, when I was preparing the column of her annual forecasts for the year ahead. "John Foster Dulles," she said, "will not be in the Cabinet after the middle of the year."

Amused by her lack of political perspicacity, I replied: "I'm not going to put that in the column. President Eisenhower relies on Mr. Dulles more than on any other member of his Cabinet. He would not dream of letting him go."

"No," she said imperturbably, "he won't discharge him."

"Well, Mr. Dulles certainly won't quit," I argued. "All of his life he has wanted to be Secretary of State."

Disregarding my show of irritation, Jeane responded: "No, he will not want to quit, but he won't be living by midyear."

Shocked, I said that I could not write such a dire prediction about a vigorous, healthy man, and in her gentle way she replied that it was up to me what I wrote; she merely told me what she foresaw.

I finally compromised. In the syndicated column of 1959 predictions, dated December 28, 1958, I wrote: "Jeane Dixon forecasts that Secretary of State Dulles, reluctantly and against his will, will retire from the Cabinet before the year's end." Before filing the column on the press wires I telephoned syndicate editor Milton Kaplan in New York, then told him what her prediction actually was and asked him to remember it in the event that she was correct. A few weeks later the State Department announced that Secretary Dulles was suffering from cancer. On May 24, 1959, he died.

CHAPTER
11

WHEN I first met Jeane Dixon I was highly skeptical of her alleged prophetic powers. As a trained newspaper writer I was accustomed to dealing in facts, and I therefore wrote the columns of her predictions lightheartedly, in a spirit of whimsey, and paid scant attention when, as I was preparing the original column in 1952, she told me: "A racial crisis will erupt in America during 1963 and will become so serious in 1964 that fighting will break out in the streets." Because this possibility seemed rather remote at the time, and my column had wide circulation in New York's Harlem and other race-conscious areas, I deliberately made no mention of that particular forecast, except to my editor. Each succeeding year Jeane tenaciously repeated the warning, however, and in 1958 I finally included her forecast that one of the tensest periods in American history would come in 1964, but I omitted the fact that she referred to a struggle between blacks and whites.

Jeane says that her first vision of future racial strife came while she was kneeling in Sacred Heart Cathedral, on Hollywood's Sunset Strip, as a child. She did not at that time see the beginning of the strife, only the "glorious ending" of the trouble between the races in approximately 1980.

"I saw the vision for the second time in 1948, while kneeling in St. Matthew's Cathedral in Washington," she continues. "This time I was shown the beginning of serious rioting in 1963, with the situation worsening in 1964. I saw colored people walking on the tops of government buildings, which were merely the symbols for authority and politics. I saw the Negroes being pushed by an underground force—shoved upwards before they were ready. They were being used by others for selfish ends, and a voice told me that not until about 1980 would peace finally come. That is God's will, and we will pay the price if we try to thwart it by pushing too fast. The racial issue will continue to dominate the decade of the 1960s, with the colored people seeking equal powers and jobs before they have the intellectual capacity and understanding to accept equal responsibility."

When Jeane speaks of the colored race, she does so with love in her heart. For the past twenty years she has contributed heavily to the support of several generations of Negroes who live at Peace Plantation, a charitable venture in Sterling, Virginia. She makes frequent trips to the farm, taking clothing and food for the men, women, and children; paying their medical and dental bills. She has bought the children their first dance dresses and suits, driven them personally to Washington dentists and eye doctors, given them jobs, and showered them with affectionate understanding. She says of these families: "I'm more indebted to them than they could ever be to me, because I have learned so much from them. We are all equal in the eyes of God."

Jeane is greatly admired by Elder Lightfoot Solomon Michaux, the pastor of a tremendous Negro congregation at Washington's Church of God and of six other churches in cities from New York to Virginia. He often introduces her as "my people's Joan of Arc." The Dixons dine occasionally at his home, and when business prevented Jimmy Dixon from attending one of Elder Michaux's recent birthday parties there, Jeane took Eleanor Bumgardner in his stead. During dinner the Elder boasted that no one knew his age. "I'm going to challenge my Washington audience tonight to touch their fingers to the floor as many times as I do, without bending their knees," he chuckled. "If anyone can defeat me I'll tell my correct age, but no one ever accepts the challenge."

Jeane, thinking he was jesting, said that she would be glad to challenge him. Nothing more was said on the subject until the group arrived at the church, which was already filled to overflowing with Elder Michaux's devoted flock. Then the old man announced from the stage that after some music by the choir Mrs. Dixon would challenge him to a contest. Jeane was appalled. Turning to Miss Bumgardner, she whispered: "Do you suppose Elder Michaux is serious? I don't know whether I can even touch the floor once." She went out to the rest room, kicked off her shoes, and swung forward. To her immense relief her fingers touched the floor. She had no sooner returned to her seat than the aging dignitary appointed a referee and summoned her on stage. He peeled off his coat, and Jeane, who was wearing a long black evening dress, shed her white lace bolero and black silk pumps.

The marathon began. Up and down they bent, five times, ten times, fifty, seventy, eighty, a hundred times. The elderly Negro began missing the floor occasionally with his fingers, but he gamely swung on until the count reached one hundred and thirty-five. Then he pantingly called a halt, exclaiming: "Is she made of rubber?" The referee asked him to tell his age, but Elder Michaux laughingly pronounced the contest a draw.

Only once in her life has Jeane Dixon seemingly failed to name the correct winner of a presidential race. Oddly enough this apparent slip-up occurred in 1960, although since 1952 she had been correctly forecasting that a blue-eyed Democrat would be elected in 1960 and would be assassinated. In my New Year's column for that January Jeane said that John F. Kennedy would not be elected the following November. She still believes that he was not. In August 1960 she wrote: "The symbol of the presidency is directly over the head of Vice-President Nixon, but a small, old-fashioned scale behind Nixon in the crystal ball can be interpreted two ways: that justice will prevail under divine guidance for Nixon or else, like the scale I saw with Mr. Truman in 1948, it means that unless the Republican party really gets out and puts forth every effort it will be toppled."

A few days before the November election Jeane excitedly rushed over to tell me that changes were occurring in the presidential scene depicted in her crystal ball. "I still see Nixon in the right half of the ball, which means victory, and Kennedy in the left," she explained, "but the bisecting line between them is not quite closed at the bottom. Through that tiny space I see little feelers, like snakes, crawling from the left side into the right."

Never having seen anything but clear glass in a crystal ball myself, I naturally did not understand what she was talking about, until she explained: "It means that unless the Republicans police every poll the victory will be stolen from them." She took out a pencil, drew a circle to represent her crystal ball, and marked a vertical line down the center. On the left side she sketched dark clouds completely surrounding a small balloon, and within the balloon a star. On the right side she drew a chair, with a circle representing Nixon just above it. I noticed that she had not brought the vertical line quite to the bottom of the circle, and within that small gap she indicated five snakes crawling over into the right side of the circle.

"Here is the presidential chair, but I don't see Nixon sitting in it," she said. "The snake heads are dropping off,

which means that Democratic intrigue in five separate poll-
ing areas will rob Nixon of his rightful victory. This is very
serious. I can't see Nixon getting it. Kennedy will sit in that
presidential chair, but something terrible will happen to
him. He simply cannot break through these dark clouds that
surround him. Look, he's a shining star inside this balloon,
but suddenly the balloon will burst and he will be gone."

The next day Jeane and Jimmy lunched with a top-
ranking official of the Republican National Committee, for
whom Jeane drew the same picture and sounded the identical
warning to "police the polls." The following Tuesday Kennedy defeated Nixon by the narrowest margin in modern
history. Election fraud was charged in several precincts, including Cook County, Illinois, and Texas, but Mr. Nixon
chose not to demand a recount. Therefore we may never
know whether Jeane Dixon actually erred in 1960, but she
says of that election: "My crystal ball clearly shows that
Nixon won but that the prize was stolen from him by certain
dishonest vote counters. The old-fashioned scale of justice
was on Nixon's side in the crystal ball, and it never disappeared even after the snakes of intrigue crawled through the
gap."

Justice Mitchell returned to work at the James L. Dixon
Agency, looking tanned and relaxed after a vacation. Jeane,
bumping into him as she was leaving the office, compli-
mented him on his appearance, and he heartily responded: "I
never felt better in my life." Jeane was on her way to a
beauty salon on Connecticut Avenue and was soon relaxing
under a drier when a vision appeared before her half-closed
eyes. The import was clear and imperative. Thrusting aside
the drier, she rushed to the telephone on the appointment
desk, dialed her office, and told salesman George Miller: "Do
as I say immediately and don't waste time asking questions.
Call an ambulance and get Mr. Mitchell to the hospital. He's
having a heart attack."

The startled salesman pivoted so that he could see Mitchell, who was calmly working at his desk in the adjoining room. Was the boss's wife wacky? Shrugging a bit, he replied: "Why, he's all right, Mrs. Dixon. I can see him from here . . . oh, my God, he's dying!" In that split second Mitchell had slumped to the floor unconscious. Struck dumb by shock, Miller limply handed the telephone to Patricia Crist, who obeyed Jeane's crisp injunction to "call an ambulance for Mr. Mitchell."

As soon as Jeane's pin curls could be undone she hastened back to find the office in an uproar and Miller complaining that "the doctor thinks I'm a kook." The ambulance had arrived promptly, and Mr. Mitchell was so near death that an oxygen mask had to be put over his face before he could be carried out on a stretcher. The doctor asked Miller how long he had known that Mitchell was sick before he called an ambulance, and the shaken man had responded: "We didn't know it at all. Mrs. Dixon telephoned from the beauty parlor to say he was dying." The doctor looked pityingly at Miller, as if he considered him a fit subject for the man with the net.

For five days Mitchell lay under an oxygen tent, while the hospital was besieged with calls. Jeane's premonition about his heart attack had made the front pages of the Washington newspapers, and Mitchell was Man of the Week. When he was at last able to receive callers, he humbly took Jeane's hand and confessed: "I want to tell you that I was never sure before, but since this happened I know that there is a God." Doctors reported that Mr. Mitchell's pulse had stopped by the time he reached the hospital. Had his attack been discovered routinely a few minutes after Jeane's call, he could not have been revived.

Employees at the Dixon realty office are well aware that their boss writes music in his spare time and that one of his compositions, "The District of Columbia Is My Home

Town," is played frequently at civic events in Washington, but few of them know how he happened to develop this hobby. As a bride, Jeane had frequently offered to read for her husband, but Jimmy was always too busy. At least, that was the excuse he gave, but she finally cornered him, brought out her crystal ball, and watched with interest as symbols formed before her eyes. "Why, Jimmy," she exclaimed, "you can write music! You can write both the melody and the lyrics."

Dixon, who had halfheartedly played the violin as a boy, scoffed: "Why, I can't write music, Jeane. People would laugh."

"What difference does that make," she persisted, "so long as you are developing a talent that God gave you? You're in harmony with the universe in this channel, and you can bring joy to other people through music. The highest honor and greatest satisfaction that you will ever know will come through your song writing."

It was shortly afterward that Jeane's father died and she flew to California for his funeral. Returning by train, she sat in the diner opposite a teen-aged boy who kept brushing away tears, and when Jeane sympathetically asked the trouble, he said that he was en route to Washington to meet his father, who was an army colonel. "I'm engaged to a girl back home in Omaha," he blurted, "but because I'm not eighteen yet I have to have my parents' consent to get married, and Dad won't give it."

To cheer him up, Jeane soothed: "Don't worry about it. My husband will compose a song for you to send to your girl. Give me your address in Washington, and I'll see that you get a copy." The army colonel and Jimmy Dixon both met the train, and as the lad followed his father down the platform, Jeane could see that he was crying again. Relating the incident to Jimmy, she asked him to help her keep the promise. That is how he happened to compose, "There's a Sweetheart in Nebraska," which was published by Shapiro, Bernstein and Company.

Fired by the immediate success of his first musical venture, Jimmy continued to compose songs and to sing them in his rich baritone at parties. He became active in musical associations and was named co-director and chairman of the John Philip Sousa Memorial. More recently he was appointed to the executive committee of the John F. Kennedy Cultural Center, for which the Sousa memorial fund is endowing the shell. On July 26, 1964, the American Bandmasters Association presented James Lamb Dixon with the Edwin Franko Goldman Memorial Award, at a Marine Band concert at the Watergate, and afterward official and social Washington gathered at the home of Mrs. Martin Vogel for a party in his honor. Another of Jeane's prophecies had come true.

Dr. F. Regis Riesenman, a psychiatrist who for fifteen years served on the psychiatric staff at St. Elizabeth's Hospital, is one of Mrs. Dixon's enthusiastic admirers. Dr. Riesenman's hobby is exposing phony mediums, and when he happened to meet Jeane at a party in May 1961 he was eager to question the woman about whom he had heard so much.

Dr. Riesenman, who performs magic tricks for the amusement of friends, staged a demonstration, and Jeane watched for a time before going to the kitchen to help their hostess with dinner preparations. While she was gone he asked each of the others to write something on a piece of paper, fold it twice, and hand it to him. He then correctly told what each of them had written. The guests were baffled, and when Jeane eventually returned to the living room they told her that she had missed the best stunt of all. Says Dr. Riesenman: "To my utter amazement she walked across the room, told what I had been doing, and then whispered in my ear the explanation of how I did it. No one else had ever guessed that trick of mine, and she hadn't even seen it performed."

Dr. Riesenman made the headlines in June 1960 when he brought Peter Hurkos, a much-publicized Dutch psychic, to Washington to help solve the eighteen-month-old murder of Mr. and Mrs. Carroll Jackson and their two little daughters. Hurkos, after visiting the scene of the crime, led police to a trash collector, who was thereupon committed for observation at his wife's request. All Washington was talking of the sensational development the next day, and everyone except Jeane seemed relieved that a dangerous murderer was no longer stalking the countryside. To business acquaintances and friends she stoutly insisted: "They've picked up the wrong man. The murderer is a musician. He's tall and has dark bushy hair." Ten days later the FBI arrested a young jazz musician from Hyattsville, Maryland, whose diary seemed to describe how the lurid crime had been committed. Jeane was confident that this time the police had the right man. He exactly fitted her description, and he has since been convicted of the murders.

Dr. Riesenman and his wife continued to see Jeane from time to time after their first encounter. Dining together in the summer of 1963, the conversation turned to Peter Hurkos, and Jeane sat quietly for a time before pensively remarking: "Mr. Hurkos has a wonderful gift from God, but I see that he is heading for difficulty. He will get into trouble before long and will go through severe emotional trials and tribulations before he sees the light."

In October 1963 Dr. Riesenman took Jeane to meet Hurkos, while he was briefly in Washington. "Hurkos had just been divorced and seemed emotionally upset," the psychiatrist says. "I drove Jeane home afterward and she told me: 'Peter Hurkos is headed for a disaster within the next couple of months.'" Two months later the Dutch psychic whose life had previously been portrayed in a two-part network television series was charged in Wisconsin with impersonating an FBI agent. The police reported that an arsenal of guns which he claimed were necessary to his police work was found in his car.

Six weeks after a pretty government employee disappeared from her Washington apartment in August of 1964, her distrait parents appealed to Dr. Riesenman for help in finding her. The FBI had already circulated her name and description as a "missing person," to no avail. It was as if the earth had swallowed the attractive young woman. The noted psychologist says he asked Hurkos to use his psychic powers to help locate her, "but all he could get was that she was still living."

On November 16, 1964, Dr. Riesenman flew to New York with Jeane Dixon, who was to be a featured guest on the Les Crane TV show. During the flight he mentioned the puzzling disappearance of the girl and Jeane asked if he had a picture of her. All that he had with him was a negative, but after Jeane meditated briefly on that she said: "She is alive. Her physical condition is satisfactory, but she is very sick emotionally and is trying to lose her identity. She is living under an assumed name in the New York area." On December 27, 1964, the missing girl telephoned her parents, asking if they would send her a plane ticket to return home. She was then in Los Angeles, but at the family reunion on New Year's Eve she confessed that she had been living in New York until early in December under the alias of Smith. Jeane had been right on every count.

Dr. Riesenman told this writer that he considers Mrs. Dixon to be "one of the two or three greatest psychics of our times, because she keeps her channels clear and never commercializes her God-given talent."

CHAPTER
12

In my New Year's column of predictions for 1962, Jeane sounded a warning that cabinet officers should be "extremely careful in their appointments to a lower echelon of government, lest a tragic situation result." Within a few months Congress launched an investigation into the free-wheeling activities of Billie Sol Estes, a thirty-seven-year-old Texan who was indicted on charges of fraud, conspiracy, and interstate transportation of fraudulent mortgages having to do with federal grain storage.

During the investigation it was charged that Estes had bought gifts for three Agriculture Department officials: Emery E. Jacobs of the Stabilization and Conservation Service; Dr. James T. Ralph, an Assistant Secretary of Agriculture; and William E. Morris, Ralph's assistant. The Agriculture Department subsequently dismissed Jacobs and Ralph. To add to Administration embarrassment, Assistant Secretary of Labor, Jerry R. Holleman resigned, after disclosing that he had received a thousand-dollar gift from Estes. Jeane's prophecy therefore proved correct, and the Billie Sol Estes case figured prominently in Senator Barry Goldwater's presidential campaign against the Administration in 1964. Later, three high-ranking Pentagon officials were indicted on charges of embezzling Defense Department funds between May 1961 and November 1963.

For that 1962 column Jeane also forecast: "Russia will beat us to the moon, but not while Soviet Premier Khrushchev and President Kennedy are still in power. Russia has already failed in several secret attempts to put a man on the moon and will suffer many other reverses before eventually succeeding. Russia does not want war, because it is making the progress it wishes without it, and as time goes by we will find ourselves allied with Russia against Red China, parts of Africa, and the Far East.

"Russia will continue to be extremely powerful through 1962, but the steady rise of Red China thereafter will coincide with deep trouble within the United States. Powerful pressure groups here will pull the President this way and that. Some are infiltrated with Communists and will plunge America into serious racial strife during the next two years. This will cause a radical change in our way of life." Year after year Jeane was stressing the danger from Red China and the forthcoming race riots in the United States.

Of President Kennedy she wrote: "It seems as though he is being surrounded by mob after mob, with no escape. As a Vice-President he would be truly great for our country and the world, but his timing was off for the leadership at this time. His vibrations are of such short wave length that they do not take hold. He will be idolized by those under him, but I am sorry to say that he will not succeed in that which he wishes to do for America." Among her other predictions were these: "Religion will play a more important role in 1962 than the public now thinks." (The Supreme Court outlawed prayer in the public schools on June 25, 1962, and a public outcry resulted.) "Richard M. Nixon will run for the governorship of California, but I do not see him winning." (He ran, and lost.)

Of the then Vice-President, Lyndon B. Johnson, she wrote: "In my meditation I do not get him as a natural originator, but he will execute with great success things which others have failed to finish. He could be a victim of circumstances. He must always stay close to his medical advisers and never depend on the advice of just one doctor." When Mr. Johnson subsequently became President he cajoled through Congress an astonishing array of legislation which had originated with his predecessor but had been stalled in committees. Again the curtain of the future had apparently parted for Jeane.

In the early fall of 1962 she telephoned to report that she had foreseen a coming event in her crystal ball: "German Chancellor Konrad Adenauer will retire late next year." Since this news was scarcely earth-shaking, I asked her to hold the forecast until we collaborated on our New Year's column in late December. By that time the Grand Old Man of West Germany had publicly announced that he had decided not to seek re-election in the fall of 1963, and the usually sweet-tempered Mrs. Dixon was patently annoyed that Chancellor Adenauer had not waited until spring for the announcement, "in order to give our column a break."

Other New Year's predictions included this one: "In 1963 America will be a more confused nation than it has been. The year will see a beginning of the decline of influence of many Ivy League colleges, and non-Ivy League colleges will come into greater prominence and importance." At the time, this seemed distinctly farfetched to me. Harvard was then riding high. A distinguished alumnus sat in the White House, and practically every top presidential appointee seemed to be a graduate of an Eastern university. Nonetheless, the man who became President that November was a graduate of Southwest Texas State Teachers' College, and as the Texas drawl began to replace the Boston twang in the

White House executive wing, the Ivy League alumni lost their predominance. Furthermore Hubert Humphrey, the man whom President Johnson selected as his running mate the following year, was an educational product of the Denver College of Pharmacy, the University of Minnesota, and the University of Louisiana.

Jeane made another strange prediction for that column, saying: "In 1963 my symbol for education is like a fashion parade. Therefore I will say that education will be the fashionable topic of conversation throughout the country." Whether "fashionable" was the correct word is debatable, but the symbol was certainly right, because the year was not far advanced before practically everyone in the nation was talking about education, thanks to the riots which flared as the government sought to enforce the integration of schools. Jeane had foreseen the race rioting ten years before, and pinpointed the timing.

The column for 1963 forecast that U.S. agriculture would continue to be the world's most productive but that our surpluses would "create a major problem." Both Russia and Red China suffered severe crop failures that year, and controversy raged throughout the nation when President Kennedy decided to sell surplus wheat to Russia and its European satellites. Jeane foresaw "a great danger signal hanging over the European Community" and said that "the Common Market paths lead into a dangerous trap." In mid-January 1963, French President Charles de Gaulle rocked the West by vetoing British entry into the Common Market.

"De Gaulle's France will be a keen competitor instead of an ally in 1963," Jeane warned. "De Gaulle will let America know that he and France are not going to be dictated to by our country, but he should guard against a personal stubborn streak. He will remain the unchallenged leader of France throughout the year, and he is moving in a direction more and more in opposition to U. S. policy. West Germany will make peaceful overtures toward East Germany, after a more flexible Chancellor succeeds Adenauer late in 1963. West Germany will lean in the same direction with France, and De Gaulle will make some headway toward a Franco-Russian rapprochement."

In late January, France and Germany signed a two-power treaty of mutual co-operation, and De Gaulle continued throughout the year to buck our foreign policies. France and Russia refused to pay their share of principal and interest on the United Nations bonds, and West Germany arranged with East Germany to permit its citizens to visit relatives in East Berlin during the Christmas season. This was an unprecedented action.

Jeane said that 1963 would mark a break between Russia and Red China, and that within a few years thereafter Red China would invade the Soviet Union with a new kind of warfare. "It looks like germ warfare," she said, "and when that time comes America and Russia will mobilize on the same side to meet the common peril. In the months ahead Russia will begin a marked shift from an Asiatic to a European nation, although Khrushchev will continue to employ many tricks to confuse the issue, while he gains time for these adjustments." The estrangement between Red Russia and Red China is now history, but whether the invasion and re-alignment which Jeane foresees will actually occur remains shrouded for the rest of us.

One of her predictions for that year seems to have been a miss. She said that America would call in some hidden money abroad, requiring it to be brought back here and exchanged for new money. Nothing of the sort developed, and when I subsequently asked her about this, she replied: "My symbols are never wrong, but sometimes I misinterpret them. I still see those symbols about money returning from abroad, and something curious will happen in that respect." She also forecast that "the South will enjoy a terrific economic boom during the years immediately ahead, and racial strife will become more pronounced throughout the country."

"The Republican party will make great strides in the South," she added. "It will put forth tremendous efforts to come closer to the people, and will thereby defeat the Democratic party in six years." If this latter prophecy comes true, a GOP victory will occur in 1968.

Frankie Welch was teaching sewing at the Washington and Lee High School in Arlington, Virginia, in 1960, when Jeane met her for the first time and chided: "You're not beginning to realize your potential. You should be in designing. I see that you will win some kind of an award soon, and if you go into designing you will make a great success of it." Shortly afterward Mrs. Welch was named "Outstanding Home Economics Teacher of the Nation" by *Ingenue* magazine, which rewarded her with a free trip to Paris and Rome to visit the great fashion houses. Jeane continued to encourage her to make designing a career, and in March 1964 a magazine devoted two full pages to pictures of the "Frankie," an all-purpose dress designed by Frankie Welch. The accompanying text read in part: "What the 'Lily' was to Palm Beach and the international Jet Set, the 'Frankie' dress is to Washington area women. It's at home in Alexandria, Georgetown, or on Embassy Row."

Mrs. Welch, who also designed some dresses for Jeane, recalls: "One day I was fitting and pinning a dress to her size eight figure, with that tiny waist, when she remarked that jackets would be fuller next year. I paid little attention, but when the French designs were unfurled at the Paris openings the trend was as Jeane had foreseen. This is just one of many examples. I have discovered that knowing Jeane is like having a pipeline to advance styles. She invariably foresees style trends."

Jeane was ordering some clothes from Mrs. Welch in 1962,

when a vision flashed before her eyes and she exclaimed: "Oh, Frankie, the most fabulous thing is going to happen to you. You're going to have a dress shop of your own in the near future. I can see it now. It will be located in an old, old house—but very chic." Mrs. Welch said she had absolutely no intention of owning a shop of her own. She had been teaching for eighteen years, and her husband was a Congressional liaison officer for the Veterans' Administration. They were too comfortable to gamble. Nevertheless, in September 1963 Frankie and her husband, Bill Welch, opened an exclusive specialty shop called "Frankie Welch of Virginia." It is located in a two-hundred-year-old Alexandria house which once housed the first bank of Virginia, where George Washington was a stockholder. "Chic" is the right word for such a setting.

"We were scared to death at taking such a step," Mrs. Welch recalls, "but Jeane told us that it would succeed beyond our wildest dreams. It has. Bill and I set ourselves a five-year goal of sales, which we passed within the first six months."

Philip Hulitar, the internationally known couturier, says that he was about to make the mistake of his life when Hope Ridings Miller providentially introduced him to Jeane Dixon in 1964. Ailing for sometime with recurrent pneumonia, he had decided that he would give up his lucrative dress designing business in Manhattan and retire to Florida's balmier climate. At six o'clock one morning, shortly after meeting Jeane, he says that she telephoned him and said, "You are faced with one of the most important decisions of your life. You are not to do anything about it for two months, because you are at a vital crossroads. Stay in New York and hold everything in abeyance."

Hulitar had just returned from Palm Beach, where he had made an offer on an expensive house, but at Jeane's insist-

ence he telephoned to cancel the bid. He waited the prescribed two months' period and then returned to Palm Beach
to look for investment property. He found something to his
liking, and had arranged a 9:30 A.M. appointment to sign
the purchase papers. At 7 A.M., the telephone rang. It was
Jeane calling. "Don't do what you're thinking about," she
urged. "I get psychically that you intend to sign some papers
today, but you must make no business deals at this time.
Personal matters are all right, but wait at least a month for
any investment property."

Hulitar was flabbergasted. Twice she had sensed his deals
just before he made them; twice intervened at the eleventh
hour. He subsequently told Mrs. Loy Anderson of Palm
Beach: "My wife and I have since discovered that if we had
signed for that building it would probably have wiped us out
financially. Jeane literally saved our bank account."

Shortly thereafter the designer received nationwide publicity when Robert F. Kennedy leased the Hulitar estate on
Long Island. Hulitar's designing business is flourishing, and
he is viewing the future optimistically, because Jeane has told
him that he will "invent someting which is so important to
women that you will make a vast fortune." He has no reason
to doubt her prophecy.

Patricia Headley was accompanying Jeane to New York for
a guest appearance on the Johnny Carson show in early 1964,
and as the airplane taxied out toward the end of the Washington runway for take-off, Jeane said: "Pat, I feel very uneasy about this plane." Aware that Jeane had once saved her
husband's life by begging him not to fly in a plane which
crashed, Pat became rather alarmed, but Jeane told her to be
calm. They sat at the end of the runway for some minutes,
with the four motors busily whirring. Then the big plane
taxied back to the terminal, and a stewardess announced over
the loudspeaker that the plane had developed a little engine

trouble. The two women changed their reservations, and as soon as they were airborne Pat asked if they would land safely.

"Oh yes, we're going to have a nice trip," Jeane replied. "Outside of Philadelphia it will get quite rough, and we'll have to fasten our seat belts, but we'll arrive safely." Just outside the Quaker City, Pat recalls, the Fasten Seat Belt sign flashed on and the plane was heavily buffeted, but they reached New York on schedule.

Early in 1963 I was riding in a taxicab along Massachusetts Avenue, when the cab driver remarked: "See that intersection we're approaching, with the stop-and-go light? And see that high hedge running almost to the street?" Absorbed in a newspaper, I barely glanced up; but he was not to be ignored. He swung around in the seat and asked: "Have you ever heard of a lady named Jeane Dixon?" I acknowledged that I knew her, and he continued: "One day she was riding where you are in this cab, and when we were about a block away from this intersection she suddenly warned me to slow up and stop before crossing that street. I told her I had the green light, but she said, 'That makes no difference. A car will come out of that cross street and run through the red light.' Well, would you believe it, if I hadn't done what she said we'd have been hit broadside by a car. A woman driver came barreling through that red light without stopping."

Intrigued, I asked him to retrace our path for two blocks. We checked it carefully. At no point was there an open space where Jeane could have glimpsed another car on the hidden side street. Even if there had been, who could have guessed that the driver would fail to stop for a red light?

In the fall of 1963, Jeane dropped in at the Washington home of her friend Marcella duPont and found her in an agitated state. Mrs. duPont said she had just telephoned her attorney to alert the insurance company, because some valuable jewels had been stolen. Meditating a moment, Jeane contradicted: "No, they were not stolen. I see those pieces of jewelry in the same case where you yourself put them. They have not been touched by anyone else."

Marcella, who had just reopened her house after a summer at Nantucket, argued that Jeane was mistaken. "I had them with me there," she said, "but they have simply disappeared. We've had a number of workmen here the last few days, and someone must have taken them. The maid and I have searched the house."

The insurance company, after due investigation, paid the claim. In January, packing for a trip to South America, Mrs. duPont went to the chest where out-of-season accessories were stored. As she was lifting out summer scarves and pocketbooks to take with her, she wondered why one of the purses felt so heavy, and upon looking inside discovered the satin case with her missing jewels.

"The memory came back to me then," Marcella says. "I had never done such a thing before, but one evening I came in late from a dinner in Nantucket and tucked the jewels into the purse until morning. We were returning to Washington almost immediately, and the maid obviously did not notice the weight of the purse when she packed my belongings in the steamer trunk to ship here." The insurance company gratefully received its refund.

CHAPTER
13

DEPUTY Assistant Secretary of State Lee Walsh met Jeane near the end of World War II. Mrs. Walsh, then a writer on women's activities for the Washington *Daily News,* sat next to Jeane at a fashion showing of women's hats, and afterwards went to her house for dinner. Jeane read for her and prophesied: "Your career will take an upswing into a different field when you are thirty years old. From that time on your income will steadily rise. In your middle or late forties I see a lot of travel for you, much of it abroad. These trips will be taken in connection with your work, which will be in the field of international relations."

Mrs. Walsh recalls that her husband was out of town that day, and Jeane had never met him, but: "She described Hal exactly to me. She said he was large, had slightly reddish hair, and fingernails that turned up at the corners. I knew the rest of it was true, but I had frankly never noticed his hands. She said that Hal and I had met at a resort, and this certainly was correct. I was vacationing at Virginia Beach shortly before Pearl Harbor, when we met and fell in love. Hal was an army private, and by the time our wedding date was set he was uncceremoniously ordered to the Pacific theater of combat instead. I was a recent bride the night that Jeane dipped into my past and future."

A few days later, when Hal Walsh returned from New York, Lee made it a point to examine his hands. Sure enough, although most people's fingernails turn down toward the cuticles at the corners, Hal's curled upward.

Lee Walsh continued in newspaper work until she was thirty. Then, receiving a much more remunerative offer, she went to work for Julius Garfinckel and Company, Washington's leading specialty store, as director of advertising and promotion. Later she returned to newspaper work as woman's page editor of the Washington *Star*, and in her forty-seventh year President Johnson appointed her Deputy Assistant Secretary of State for Evaluations, a post which has kept her traveling abroad almost constantly ever since.

By the decade of the 1960s Jeane had become so widely known that mail from Europe and Asia, addressed simply to "Jeane Dixon, U.S.A.," was promptly delivered to her door. My annual columns about her predictions were syndicated here and abroad, and each time one appeared Jeane and I both received an avalanche of mail from readers who wanted her to help solve their problems or simply to foretell their future. She always returned the checks and cash that frequently accompanied these pleas. If a particular query touched a psychic chord, she sometimes included a word of caution or advice in responding to the letters, but more often she autographed a card, printed at her own expense, which read:

> I know not by what methods rare,
> But this I know—God answers prayer.
> I know not when He sends the word
> That tells us fervent prayer is heard.
> I know it cometh—soon or late;

Therefore we need to pray and wait.
I know not if the blessing sought
Will come in just the way I thought.
I leave my prayers with Him alone,
Whose will is wiser than my own.

Anonymous

Because Jeane is so acutely sensitive to the suffering and worries of others, she finds it necessary to protect herself by avoiding too close contact with those who would burden her with their problems. A full-time secretary is required simply to handle her "psychic" mail, and the postage is a sizable budget item, since few of her unknown correspondents are thoughtful enough to enclose stamped envelopes.

Mrs. Coya Knutson was a U.S. congresswoman from Minnesota when she first met Mrs. Dixon in the spring of 1956, at the same party where Jeane warned Estes Kefauver that he would have to settle for second place on the Democratic ticket. Jeane was reading for several of the guests, and when Mrs. Knutson's turn came she looked into her crystal ball and told her: "Your husband is going to defeat you for re-election." At that time few people in Washington had even heard of Coya's husband, who had remained in Minnesota, but Mrs. Knutson listened intently while Jeane added: "You had better do something about this domestic situation before it's too late."

The former congresswoman now says of that confrontation with Jeane: "I was well aware of my home problem, but I wondered how a stranger could so readily probe into my own fears about my career. I sensed that she was right, but I was then working hard in behalf of a bill that had been my prime reason in running for Congress, so I delayed action on my domestic situation."

Mrs. Knutson's bill was eventually successful, but her Congressional career simultaneously came to the abrupt end that

Jeane had foreseen. For sixteen years before coming to Congress, Coya had taught English and music in a Minnesota high school. For four of those years she also served in the state legislature. Deeply interested in education, she decided to run for Congress in order to sponsor an education act that would provide student loans. In the small communities of her Minnesota district she had sadly observed the number of worthy students who were forced by lack of funds to drop out of college. She won election in November 1954, was re-elected two years later, and in August 1958 saw her bill become a reality as Title II of the National Defense Education Act.

President Eisenhower signed it into law on September 2, and Representative Carl Elliott, chairman of the Subcommittee on Special Education, wrote a letter to Mrs. Knutson praising her contribution to the bill. Unfortunately, by this time Mrs. Knutson had also received the highly publicized "Coya, come home" letter written by her husband, Andy. His open letter asked her not to seek re-election. In the campaign that fall the epistle received far more publicity than her successful student loan bill, and she realized that she was fighting a losing battle. Mrs. Knutson had not seen Jeane Dixon since that evening two years before, but one day in the fall of 1958 she talked by telephone with her from campaign headquarters in Moorhead, Minnesota.

"Jeane's voice was weak and husky," Mrs. Knutson recalls. "She said she was sick in bed with a cold but wanted to tell me that she had seen a vision of me in New York with Mike the MagiCat."

"What on earth is that?" she asked in astonishment.

Jeane explained that this was the name of her pet cat, who often appeared with her on television shows, "And for some reason I have just seen you in New York with him." After Mrs. Knutson lost to her Republican opponent, she returned to Washington to close her Congressional office. It was some comfort to her that she had just received the annual award of the National Cystic Fibrosis Research Foundation for her efforts in arousing Congressional interest in this killer of America's children. "Through her fine efforts," the citation said of Coya Knutson, "research work to find a cure for cystic fibrosis will be advanced tenfold."

Meanwhile, a Hollywood studio had asked to make a pilot film about Mike the MagiCat, an engaging little black and white mongrel of questionable parentage who made newspaper headlines in February 1952. He had disappeared from the Dixon ménage, and when Jeane ran a descriptive advertisement about him in the lost-and-found columns, a White House employe telephoned to say that he had turned up on the executive mansion's front lawn. Jeane gratefully retrieved him, but two months later he was gone again. This time, suspecting that he might have retraced his steps, Jeane telephoned Estelle Friedrichs and asked if she could discreetly inquire around the White House to see if anyone had spotted him.

"I called a guard," Mrs. Friedrichs recalls, "and asked if he had seen a black and white alley cat. The guard replied that he was right there, eating the ham out of his sandwich." Mike the MagiCat was delivered in style to the Dixon residence by chauffeured limousine, with accompanying guard. By this time most of the local columnists were familiar with the quizzical little fellow, who invariably accompanied Jeane to her public appearances and stared with fascination into her crystal ball.

Knowing that Coya Knutson was unemployed, Jeane recommended her as the liaison with the film company, and as foreseen eight months before Mrs. Knutson was soon in New York chaperoning the Dixon cat. During this period Jeane told her: "Coya, I see a golden thread running all the way around the world where you are concerned. You're good for the children of the whole world." Neither of them could guess that within four years Coya would be named educational director of a new international children-to-children program.

In the summer of 1960 Coya quit her job with the film company to return home and try for re-election, although Jeane begged her not to do so, warning: "You can't win, Coya; I see the defeat in my crystal ball." Mrs. Knutson won the Democratic primary, only to lose again to the Republican incumbent. Her husband's letter was still being used against her. Out of a job, she returned to Washington in January 1961. Jeane promptly began helping her financially, and paid her tuition at a protocol school which taught grooming, poise, and governmental ins-and-outs. She divorced her husband in 1962 and soon thereafter found a job as Congressional liaison officer for Civilian Defense.

She flew with Jeane to Cleveland in the spring of 1964 for an appearance on the Mike Douglas TV show, and says of the experience: "Jeane looked beautiful, as usual, although she was not feeling well. She was introduced to Margaret Whiting, and as soon as they shook hands Jeane told her, 'You ought to write a book about your father. You and your father had a lot in common. You both were born with musical talent.' " As soon as Coya could get Jeane alone, she asked if she knew the identity of the young woman to whom she had given that advice. Jeane had no idea. Mrs. Knutson then explained that she was a prominent television singer and that her father, the late Richard Whiting, had composed such hit tunes as "On the Good Ship Lollipop," "I Can't Escape from You," and "When You're Smiling."

Jeane's introduction to Mike Douglas was equally offbeat. She had never met him, but when she touched his fingertips she exclaimed: "When you were a youngster you were so bashful and frightened that you wanted to hide when people came around. If they asked you to sing, you used to go in the next room so that they couldn't see you." The extroverted Mr. Douglas seemed flabbergasted as he replied: "How on earth could you know that? You're absolutely right. I was painfully bashful as a child."

Jeane is accustomed to taking her interviewers by surprise. I once heard her tell a Washington television moderator: "You should patent your inventions, because they will bring you a lot of money." The startled moderator replied that until that moment no one except his wife had known that his hobby was "inventing things."

Jeane went to Boston in the early spring of 1964 to be interviewed on Bob Kennedy's ninety-minute television show. Her role was to answer questions telephoned by viewers, but the program had not yet begun when she turned to her host and advised: "You go ahead and take those singing lessons you're thinking about."

Recalling it afterwards, Mr. Kennedy told me: "So help me, not a single soul in the world except my wife knew that I was thinking about taking vocal lessons. I had thought that they might come in handy, in the event something happened to my interview program."

While Bob Kennedy was still marveling at his guest's psychic perception, she said: "You made a major change when you were twenty-eight years old that altered your career. You will make another change later on that will be equally drastic." The moderator conceded that, when twenty-eight, he had switched from being a writer-producer to being a television performer. He is now prepared for any eventuality.

Jeane is particularly adept at discovering hidden talents and career potentials in young people, through psychic means. When her niece Mary Frances Pinckert was eight years old, Jeane told her brother and sister-in-law that the child had artistic ability that should be encouraged. "One day she will make a name for herself with her paintings," she prophesied.

Since a prophet is seldom recognized at home, Mary Frances' parents did nothing to encourage the little girl to paint.

As part of her regular curriculum in junior high school she did satisfactory work in art class, but nothing more. Then California launched a contest for creative painting, and on the last evening before the deadline for submission of exhibits, Mary Frances went to her room to paint. Mrs. Pinckert discovered the fourteen-year-old girl at her easel when she took a glass of milk to her room. Mary Frances did not come to dinner. At bedtime Mrs. Pinckert looked into her room and noticed that she was still painting. The next morning she went to the room to awaken Mary Frances and found her cleaning her brushes.

"Oh, Mother, I'm just dead," the girl sighed.

Realizing for the first time that the youngster had been painting all night, Mrs. Pinckert glanced toward the easel and exclaimed in admiration as she studied the imaginary picture of a Japanese geisha girl. Mary Frances tumbled wearily into bed, but her mother rushed the picture to the framer's, waited for it, and entered it in the contest. The geisha girl took first prize and became a museum exhibit.

CHAPTER
14

UNINFORMED people who mistakenly view Jeane Dixon's psychic gift as a form of fortunetelling wonder how she manages to "remain in the good graces of the Catholic Church," which usually frowns on such endeavors. Because I am not a Catholic, I took the question to Monsignor James A. Magner, procurator of Catholic University of America, who knows her well. The monsignor said of Jeane's talent: "There is no conflict at all between that and the Church. Our religion, in fact, is largely based on visions. The Annunciation foretold the coming of Christ. At the time of the birth of our Lord angels appeared in the heavens. The Bible is replete with prophecies and visions. Christ appeared to St. Paul in a vision. The Holy Ghost descended at Pentecost. The Blessed Virgin was seen at Lourdes. Neither in idea nor expression is there any conflict between Mrs. Dixon's gift and the Church. In fact, to a Catholic it seems a rather normal thing, although we don't yet know very much about this field of psychic phenomena." Of Jeane Dixon personally, the monsignor remarked: "She is extremely devout. She is outgoing and kind, very definitely generous, and desirous of helping others.

There is not a drop of selfishness in her. She is a superior person in every way."

Jeane's most vivid recollection of the 1939-40 World's Fair is of a painting that she saw in one of the pavilions. The moment that she glimpsed Innocenzo da Imola's sixteenth-century painting of the Madonna and Child in a nativity scene, she yearned to own it. "This painting held a very special message for me," she explains. "I certainly had no place to hang it, because it was much too large for my wall; yet I sensed instantly that one day I would find the place where it belonged." However, the painting was not for sale.

Two years later Jeane was shopping in Washington for a birthday present for a friend who liked large, jangling bracelets, and though Jeane herself dislikes costume jewelry, she went to an import house that specialized in such wares. She selected a bracelet and while waiting for it to be gift wrapped happened to glance into the rear of the store. There, leaning against a wall, was the painting she had admired so deeply at the fair. Striving to sound nonchalant, she inquired about it and learned that the shopkeeper was preparing to ship it back to Europe because it was too expensive for his Washington trade; and when he mentioned the price, she could understand why. Jeane unhappily departed with her purchase but could not put the painting out of her mind. Unlocking her safe, she removed the old-fashioned jewelry that she had inherited from her mother-in-law, telephoned an art connoisseur, and commissioned him to take the jewels to the import house.

"I had noticed how longingly the shopkeeper eyed a beautiful young Iranian girl who was clerking there," Jeane reminisces, "so I asked the connoisseur to make sure that she saw the jewels when he displayed them to the owner of the store. Within a few days I had the painting, the girl had a diamond bracelet, the shopkeeper had the girl for his wife, and the art connoisseur had a handsome commission. Everyone profited by the transaction."

Jeane sensed that her husband would not approve of the exchange, however, so she told him nothing about it and arranged to store the painting at the Virginia abode of Representative Usher Burdick of North Dakota. Nearly a decade later the congressman offered to buy the painting from Jeane for $35,000. She did not want to sell, but the offer spurred her to action. Through the art connoisseur she arranged to have it brought to the attention of Monsignor Magner, who examined it and said that he would be grateful to receive the painting on behalf of Catholic University of America. Jeane agreed to make the donation if she could dedicate it to her husband.

For a year longer she kept her secret from Jimmy, while the painting was being restored. With the date finally set for the dedication, she asked Jimmy to accompany her to the university for the unveiling of a picture, but he brusquely replied that he was much too busy with real estate appointments to attend an art exhibit on a workday. "It was like pulling hen's teeth to persuade him to go," Jeane ruefully recalls. "I'd had a brass plaque made for the painting, saying that it was being presented in honor of James Lamb Dixon, but of course he knew nothing of that. I finally had to cry before I could get him to say yes. By that time he was so annoyed with me that he took a separate car, so that he could rush on to his appointments. He said he would stay exactly fifteen minutes, but when he saw the silver tea service laid out for a special event, and the impressive ceremony as Monsignor (now Bishop) William J. McDonald, wearing his flowing robe with purple sash, led the procession of prelates down the stairs Jimmy stayed two hours."

The wife of Philippine Ambassador Carlos Romulo and others of Jeane's friends watched Jimmy while the monsignor read the history of the painting. He said that the artist, Innocenzo da Imola, had lived from 1490 to 1549 and that in all of Europe there were perhaps only five of his priceless religious paintings in churches. By the time Jimmy learned that Jeane had donated the painting, and dedicated it to him, he was pale with emotion. Catholic University was so proud of its acquisition that it later exhibited the painting on a television program and reproduced its likeness on the school's official Christmas cards.

In May of 1964, at the ceremony of consecration for the Most Reverend William Joseph McDonald, the new bishop autographed a program with these words: "To Mrs. Jeane Dixon, whose deep spirituality and genuine Christian culture are sources of inspiration and edification to her many friends. With a blessing, Sincerely in Christ, William J. McDonald."

Although Jeane is a devout Roman Catholic, she is equally respectful of all religions. One who attests to this fact is the Rev. McArthur Jollay, pastor of the Full Gospel Church in Washington. The minister of the interdenominational congregation met Jeane through a business association, after his church had purchased a large lot on Massachusetts Avenue and approved plans for the construction of a $650,000 edifice with a seating capacity of sixteen hundred. Jeane evinced an interest in the project, and when he showed her the blueprints, she exclaimed: "But, Mr. Jollay, there is no place here for a little chapel where people can come and meditate. Look at these tremendous apartment buildings around here. Think of the students at American University nearby! You should have a little chapel where people who are troubled and careworn can stop in to pray at any hour."

To emphasize her point, Jeane repeated the words of a song written by her husband:

> "There's a little old church by the side of the road,
> Such a haven of rest when you're packin' a load;
> There's a little old light shinin' ever so bright

In that little old church by the side of the road.
It's God's own shrine of things divine and seems to say,
'Now if you can, Mister Travelin' Man, stop in to pray,
In that little old church by the side of the road,
Such a haven of rest when you're packin' a load.' "

The Rev. Mr. Jollay frankly acknowledges that because of her inspiration he altered the plans to include a small chapel adjacent to the sanctuary, which will be open at all times, day or night. Of Mrs. Dixon he volunteers: "She is a most interesting person! She is a Roman Catholic, but very open in her attitude toward Christianity everywhere. She is a very magnanimous lady."

CHAPTER
15

FRIENDS have learned that if they want to visit with Jeane Dixon they must catch up with her on the fly. A dynamo in motion, she works twelve-hour days, seven days a week, beginning each with attendance at Mass. She not only serves as secretary-treasurer of the James L. Dixon Realty Company, she handles all settlements and loans for its residential department, and personally sells many homes and business properties. One crisp November evening in 1963 Lorene Mason stopped by the office, in order to walk home with Jeane. Strolling along Connecticut Avenue, she mentioned a Frank Sinatra movie that she had seen, and as she did so Jeane cried out: "Lorene, Frank Sinatra is in for a terrific shock!"

"Is he going to die?" Lorene gasped.

"No, no, no," Jeane murmured, "but he's going to have a severe shock that he will remember the rest of his life. He's going to think that it's a death, but it isn't. It concerns his son. This is a situation that will bring him the greatest heartbreak of his life. Some sort of scandal is attached to it." Lorene asked how she could be sure that it was scandal, rather than death, and Jeane replied: "Because just as you said Sinatra's name a curtain came down, clear to the bottom of the sidewalk. But it was gray, not black. Black would have meant death."

Miss Mason recalls that approximately ten days later she was half listening to the "Today" show, when the newscaster announced that Frank Sinatra, Jr., had been kidnaped. She immediately telephoned Jeane, who assured her that he was alive and unharmed. He was, but when the three men accused of kidnaping him were brought to trial, defense attorneys charged that the young singer had helped to plan his own kidnaping as a hoax, to further his stage career. The charge was denied, and the men were convicted, but there is little question that Frank, Sr., suffered real heartache.

Lorene also recalls that, many months before Elizabeth Taylor married Richard Burton, she remarked to Jeane that Burton would probably never marry Liz, and Jeane responded: "Oh yes, he will. They will be married, but money will be at the root of their trouble and will delay the wedding." Jeane made a similar forcast on the Johnny Carson TV show, and as the world was soon to know, Miss Taylor's wedding was long delayed while her rejected husband, Eddie Fisher, insisted upon talking money along with divorce.

In the early spring of 1964, Jeane was lunching with Lady Bumgardner and their mutual friend Hildegarde, who had an engagement in Washington. The singer was talking about plans for the season when, with a puzzled frown creasing her forehead, Jeane interrupted to say: "It's the oddest thing, Hildegarde, but I have just seen you in nun's robes. I can't understand why, because I'm sure that you're not going to enter a convent."

The singing star merrily assured Jeane that she was right on the latter score, at least. Approximately two months later producer Charles R. Wood announced that he had signed Hildegarde for her first dramatic appearance on the legitimate stage. She would, he said, star in Christopher Blake's *Lavallière,* the story of an actress who gave up her career to enter a convent but was rejected.

Although Jeane is right most of the time, occasionally one of her psychic utterances sounds so farfetched that I omit it from my New Year's columns. One such omission was made in late December 1963; it concerned the murder of President Kennedy, of which Jeane wrote: "As I interpret my symbols, Fidel Castro believed that President Kennedy and Premier Khrushchev had gotten together on a plan to eliminate him and replace him with someone more acceptable to the United States and the U.N. Castro, in his conniving way, therefore arranged for the assassination of John F. Kennedy. Lee Harvey Oswald was the trigger man, but there were other people involved in the plot."

Oswald's mother came to Washington a short time later to testify before the Warren Commission, and at her request a lawyer arranged an interview for her with Jeane, who says of the meeting: "She wasn't exactly the type of person I had expected. I thought she would be a little on the hard-boiled side, but she was smaller than I had anticipated, and her complexion was beautiful. From her vibrations I knew that she had a very contradictory character. She loves her country but is very, very restless. She can only be quiet so long, and then must have change. She is afflicted with wanderlust. The only way she can correct this restlessness is by severe discipline. She wanted to know whether I thought her son had fired the shot that killed the President. I told her what had come to me psychically in advance: the killer's two-syllable name of five or six letters, with an *s* for the second letter. She told me she thought her son was part of the plot, but she believed that our own government was behind it. She thought no Communist intrigue was involved."

Jeane says of the case: "I got psychically that Castro was very disturbed about an 'understanding' he believed had been arrived at between Kennedy and Khrushchev regarding Cuba. He became convinced that the only way to block their plan to eliminate him was for him to beat one of them to the punch. Castro knew that he would have no opportunity to dispose of Khrushchev, so the only way to upset their applecart was for him to arrange the murder of President Kennedy." The Warren Commission has since ruled that Lee Oswald acted alone, without confederates, but some people both here and abroad refuse to accept that verdict. In this particular instance, we may never know whether Jeane was right or wrong in her interpretation of the symbols in the crystal ball.

Kay Halle, to whom Jeane first brought the warning that President Kennedy would be assassinated unless he canceled a trip South, invited Jeane to lunch at her Georgetown house on February 28, 1964. Her nephew was also present, and Jeane was warning of a health condition which President Johnson must watch, when Kay chided: "Stop it, Jeane. I just can't take any more presidential tragedies. Let's change the subject. Have you seen any pictures about other events lately?"

"Yes," Jeane replied hesitantly, "for some reason I keep seeing a picture of the earth upturning, of houses breaking up and crashing, and of great geysers of water."

"Is it nearby?" Kay asked in alarm.

"No, it isn't," Jeane assured her friend, "I see the earth shaking, but it's somewhere up in the Canada or Alaska area. It's way up northwest from here."

Two weeks later Miss Halle read of a slight earthquake in Chile and telephoned Jeane to ask if that was what she had foreseen. "No," Jeane replied emphatically. "That's in the south, and you'll remember that the one I saw was in the northwest, around Canada or Alaska. It's a great deal more shattering than the one you're talking about." On March 27, 1964, Alaska suffered one of the most destructive earthquakes of modern times. Only four weeks had elapsed since Jeane's prediction.

By midsummer of 1964 this book was well under way, and I sometimes talked with Jeane by telephone two or three times a day. On the morning of July 9, as I was preparing to fly to San Francisco to cover the Republican National Convention, I called her and said that I had a small problem. Before I could proceed she interrupted: "Yes, it's about Pepe. What would you like me to do about him?" Although by this time I was suitably impressed by her psychic powers, I was nonplused by this response. Never before had I asked her to do anything for my little French poodle, Pepe, and not until a few minutes before my call had I learned that my maid could not be there to receive him when the kennel manager delivered him on the day that I returned home. My sole reason for the call, therefore, was to ask Jeane if I could have Pepe dropped off at her house for a few hours, until my plane landed. Whether this was thought transference I do not know, but Jeane gladly assented, and I flew to the convention with a free mind.

Mrs. Ambrose Diehl, widow of a U.S. Steel vice-president, had invited me to stay with her during the convention but because I would be working long hours I declined. Not until my return a week later did I learn of another startling example of Jeane's psychic ability. The widow of Sir Wilmott Lewis, long-time Washington correspondent for the London *Times*, gave me this account: "Jeane stopped in to see me one morning, and while we were chatting I asked what she could 'get' for me. She didn't tell me anything about myself—for some reason she never does—so I changed the subject by saying that I was a little worried about Frances Diehl. She hadn't seemed too well lately, and I knew that Jeane was acquainted with her. As I mentioned Frances' name, Jeane said slowly: 'I see her drawing down a black curtain in her house. There is death around Frances, very near, although it isn't Frances herself, because she's pulling down the curtain.'"

The next day Lady Lewis learned that Mrs. Diehl had

found her house guest, Mrs. Charles Kittle, dead of a heart attack. Jane Kittle's sudden death was a severe shock to Lady Lewis and to all of us who knew her. The widow of a former president of Sears, Roebuck & Company, she had been married briefly in her youth to cartoonist Fontaine Fox, inventor of the "Toonerville Trolley" comic strip. Oddly enough, Fox himself lived only two more weeks.

The Beatles have shattered the calm of numerous American households containing teen-agers, and they inadvertently inflicted havoc on Jeane Dixon. Like the average adult, she was only vaguely aware of the Beatle phenomenon and had never meditated on the mop-haired group. Consequently she was astonished when, in March 1964, television commentators, newspaper and magazine writers from every section of the country began calling her long distance to ask about reports that she had predicted death in a plane crash for the Beatles the following August.

Bewildered by the unexpected queries, Jeane replied that she had made no predictions of any kind about the Beatles. Hundreds of teen-agers, obviously badly shaken by reports of her alleged forecast, also called, and many of them sobbed as they begged to know whether there was any way to keep the Beatles alive. Then great bags of mail began to arrive, and Jeane could scarcely sleep at night because of the ceaselessly ringing telephone. The inundation of calls and letters so seriously interfered with her workaday life that she appealed to me for advice, and I suggested that she meditate on the Beatles. If anything came to her psychically, I could then write a newspaper column relating what she actually foresaw for them. She did so, and my syndicate on March 26, 1964, carried the news that Jeane forecast continued success for the Beatles, though one of them would "unfortunately branch out from the team before long, and later regret it." The column assured Beatle fans that Mrs. Dixon foresaw no plane crash or other kind of violent death for any of the four enter-tainers. This column precipitated another deluge of letters thanking Jeane for the "good news," and several Beatle Fan Clubs in Virginia and Pennsylvania gratefully named her their Woman of the Year.

Comparative calm returned to the Dixon office until late August 1964, when again the switchboard was clogged with calls from London, Hawaii, and a score of mainland states. Was it true that Mrs. Dixon had forecast the tragic death on September 3 or 4 of three of the four Beatles? Someone who identified herself as Mrs. Louise Harrison Caldwell, a sister of "Beatle" George Harrison, called from Benton, Illinois to say that her brother was concerned about the "prediction" and wondered whether the group should cancel its appear-ance, at that time, at the State Fair in Indianapolis.

As patiently as possible Jeane again assured all callers that she foresaw nothing but good health for all four Beatles. Where, she kept asking, had the rumors started? No one seemed to know, except that inch-high headlines in the London *Daily Mail* and several other English papers re-ported the alleged forecast by Mrs. Dixon. Two days later Deputy Assistant Secretary of State Lee Walsh, who was in Great Britain at the time, air-mailed Jeane several of the London newspapers. All of the articles carried U.S. date lines, and since a bevy of London reporters was traveling with the Beatles on their American tour, it can only be as-sumed that several of them decided to jazz up their coverage with something besides shrieking teen-ager reactions.

Jeane sometimes finds herself unexpectedly involved in diplomatic intrigue, and one such incident occurred shortly after the Bay of Pigs fiasco in early 1961. A man whose name was unknown to her repeatedly called her office, asking for an appointment; but since all such requests from strangers are declined, she thought no more about it until a friend telephoned in his behalf. Jeane finally agreed to see him, and when Mario Garcia Kohly walked into her office at the appointed time she touched his fingertips and said: "You will have far more trouble raising the funds for a revolution than you will in actually getting into Cuba. You will do that several times. However, in trying to raise money for an invasion you will undergo the greatest heartbreak of your life. You will have cause to regret your action."

Garcia Kohly, in discussing the encounter with me in the fall of 1964, more than three years after the reading, said: "Mrs. Dixon was fantastically accurate. Since then I have managed to slip in and out of my native country several times without detection, but I have been far less successful in raising funds for a revolution or invasion." His jaw tightened, and he volunteered the information that he had recently been sentenced to a year's imprisonment, after a trial in the Southern District Federal Court in New York City, for counterfeiting "Castro money." It had been intended for use, he said, in infiltration of Cuba to liberate that troubled island from Communist rule, and he was then out on appeal.

He referred me to the Congressional Record of Monday, October 1, 1962, in which Representative John R. Pillion of New York inserted a proclamation signed by "the major groups of the underground now fighting in Cuba." Issued on June 20 "at a certain place in Havana," the proclamation asked that Mario Garcia Kohly be recognized by other nations as the provisional president of a Cuban de facto government in exile. In an accompanying speech Representative Pillion said that the group represented "a union of ninety-six Cuban refugee groups embracing about 118,000 refugees and 45,000 underground fighters."

Petite, feminine Jeane does not look like the sort of person who would be advising spies on underground activities, even inadvertently. However, her window-on-tomorrow seems to choose no favorites.

Margaret Arthur, a nurse in the employ of Dr. Don John-son of Washington, came to know Jeane through the latter's frequent office calls for treatment of a chronic sinus condi-tion. When she learned that I was writing a book on Mrs. Dixon, Miss Arthur voluntarily wrote me the following let-ter: "Four years ago I had a hemorrhage from a duodenal ulcer, which necessitated a lengthy hospital stay and a long period of convalescence. Shortly after leaving the hospital, I was talking to Mrs. Dixon and mentioned that I was con-cerned about my hospital bill and did not know how I would manage for the next two months. She took my hand, and after a minute told me not to worry. She said everything was going to be all right, because I would receive a sum of money soon. I laughed, because my family is not wealthy, and I would not ask them for help. When she said it would be an inheritance, I laughed again, because none of my relatives have that kind of money or are likely to include me in their wills. An elderly woman whom I knew fell and broke her hip just before I became sick. A month after I left the hospital she had a heart attack and died. When her will was read I was remembered in it, just as Jeane had told me. I then had enough money not only to pay my current expenses, but to set aside a small nest egg as well."

Russell P. Riley, a Washington realtor, recalls that one day when Mrs. Dixon was having lunch with a client she sud-denly said that she had to leave, because she felt that there was a fire which concerned her very much. She rushed to her husband's real estate office and saw firemen throwing furni-ture out of the window. "I remember," he continued, "that when columnists were writing of Lynda Bird Johnson's ap-proaching marriage after her father became President, Mrs. Dixon said she would not wed the man to whom she was then engaged. Within a few months the engagement was broken. Another time Mrs. Dixon predicted to me that a friend of hers who was having marital difficulties would try to commit suicide. Shortly thereafter, when she tried to telephone her and could get no answer, Mrs. Dixon dispatched an ambulance to her house. The doctor who answered the call said the woman had swallowed an overdose of sleeping pills and would have died except for that quick trip to the hospital."

Ira Walsh, a Hearst newspaper executive who is on loan to Director Sargent Shriver as a special assistant in the War Against Poverty program, met Jeane Dixon by fortunate chance in February of 1965. He was lunching with a business associate at the Mayflower Hotel, and on hearing his companion greet an attractive woman at an adjoining table as "Mrs. Dixon," he asked whether that was the famous Jeane Dixon he had been reading about for twelve years.

Assured that it was, he invited her to lunch a few days later. This is his account of what happened: "I was sitting there thinking what a great Hearst comic strip could be woven around her Mike the MagiCat, when she suddenly said, 'Mr. Walsh, before you discuss comic strips I want to say . . .' I did a double-take, because I hadn't even mentioned the idea. She told me a little about her life, and I began thinking what a great movie it would make, when she said, 'Before you talk about a motion picture . . .'

"At this point, I jumped up and said that the next time she read my mind I was going to walk out of the place. It was simply too eerie to feel that I couldn't even have thoughts without her knowing them. She laughingly promised not to do it again, and we shook hands on the agreement. At that point, in touching my hand she apparently picked up something out of the air, because her mood changed abruptly and she said, 'Before you walk out on me, why don't you see a doctor right away? If you do, you can greatly prolong your life.' "

Walsh says he was feeling "absolutely great," and friends had been telling him that he had never looked better since losing some weight. Jeane's remark nonetheless preyed on his mind, and the following Thursday he went to a doctor for a checkup. Since his home was in San Francisco and he had been in Washington only a few months, he was unknown to the physician, but after undergoing the usual tests he was told: "Your blood sugar count is over five hundred. It's lucky that you walked in here today, because you could have gone into shock and dropped dead if you hadn't." The doctor detained him for another hour to avoid the possibility of his passing into coma, and prescribed a rigid diet. Of this experience, Walsh says: "There is no question but that Jeane Dixon saved my life. If I had delayed seeing a doctor, I would not be here today. Although I previously was an utter disbeliever in the psychic field, now I'll even believe in ghosts."

This sixth sense of Jeane's has baffled all who know her, but because of it most of her friends turn instantly to her for advice when a major decision confronts them. Sister Mary Mercy, a nun in the Order of the Holy Names, used to have lunch with Jeane each year when she journeyed to Washington from California to visit her parents, Senator and Mrs. Pat McCarran. At the time of her father's death, however, she was living in the Hall of Study at Catholic University and working on her doctorate in art and archaeology. Sister Mary Mercy had known Jeane for many years, but because a nun does not indulge in close friendships it was a casual relationship built on mutual respect. One day in the fall of 1956, Sister Mary Mercy and two other friends lunched with Jeane, and as the women rose to leave, the nun motioned Jeane aside and said that she would like to ask her advice about something.

"I know," Jeane calmly replied, "you don't need to tell me. You want to know whether you should leave the convent." Sister Mary Mercy was astonished. To no one had she yet confided that after nearly thirty-two years she felt called to leave the convent and care for her widowed mother. Jeane had correctly read her heart. With a papal dispensation, Sister Mary Mercy renounced her vows the following year and resumed her name of Mary McCarran. Four years later I wrote a book about her convent life, entitled, *Once There Was a Nun*. During its preparation Mary told me that Jeane had divined her secret and had subsequently helped her to buy the dress, shoes, and coat for which she exchanged her nun's robes, the day that she left the convent.

CHAPTER
16

JEANE DIXON's training in nuclear science and technology is roughly equivalent to that of a kindergarten pupil. This lack of background knowledge in a field never seems to interfere with her remarkable insight, however, when she sees visions. This ability revealed itself during a meeting called by a group of scientifically trained men on August 14, 1963, for the purpose of probing extrasensory perception.

Among those present at the session held in the Washington legal offices of Haley, Bader and Potts were Dr. William Brewster, a research physicist at Walter Reed Army Hospital; Andrew Haley, general counsel for the International Astronautical Federation and counsel of the American Institute of Aeronautics and Astronautics; James Shiner, assistant to the director of biotechnology and human research, office of advanced research and technology at NASA, our space agency; Dr. F. Regis Riesenman, well-known psychiatrist; and Mr. and Mrs. Dixon.

Haley is a recognized authority on outer space who has written two books on the subject: *Rocketry and Space Exploration* and *Space Law and Government.* Hearing of Jeane

Dixon in 1953 through her nationally televised prediction that Russia would launch a satellite into orbit around the earth, he made inquiry among European scientists but could learn of no Russian space program whatsoever. Two years later, while attending the International Astronautical Federation Congress in Copenhagen, Soviet delegates told Haley that they were working on such a program.

On his return to Washington he called on Jeane to ask for further details. How had she known of such a project? Jeane hadn't. All she could tell him was that she had "seen" Russia launching the world's first satellite, that it resembled a silver ball, and that as it returned to Russia it changed into a dove that sank its claws into the scalp of a bald man who would then be the Russian leader. This information was in the back of Haley's mind while he served as a U.S. observer at international conferences on aeronautics and missiles in Germany, Belgium, Italy, and France, traveled to the UNESCO general conference in New Delhi, India, and served as president of the American Rocket Society and chairman of its space flight committee.

In 1957 when Russia launched Sputnik I, Andrew Haley was one of the first to telephone his congratulations to the amateur who had called the shot four years previously. Haley continued to consult with her from time to time and eventually arranged the meeting with her and a panel of scientists in his office six years later. "The panel examined Mrs. Dixon closely about her visions—how they came to her, how she interpreted them, and whether she had had any others concerning outer space," Haley recalls. "The most interesting thing about the evening was that, except for myself, Jeane Dixon was more knowledgeable about rockets than anyone else in the room."

Dr. Riesenman, informed of the space attorney's appraisal, affirms: "There is no question but that this is true. Although she has probably never read an article on the subject in her life, she spoke with amazing knowledge."

Because the scientists had seemed so eager to know more about the future of the space race, Jeane agreed to meditate on rockets that night. After retiring to bed, she says, a vision came to her in the darkness, lighting the bedroom. "I saw a silver ball like the sputnik rising out of Russia and going into a powerful missile which traveled around the globe to the left. Suddenly it switched course and traveled in the opposite direction. Beneath it America was all aglow, but as the missile turned, the lights of our country went out, leaving us in utter darkness. I interpreted this to mean that Russia has a secret type of missile for which we have no anti-missile missile. It is so powerful that it can completely immobilize our communications and lighting systems. It can also play havoc with the navigation of our planes."

I asked Jeane whether she meant to imply that the Soviets already have such a frightening weapon or whether she was "seeing" into the future. She said she is confident that the Russians had already developed it by the fall of 1963 "and were getting ready to let our government know that they had it, in order to force us to do business on their terms, when the assassination of President Kennedy intervened."

Seven weeks following the vision, on October 6, 1963, Jeane sounded a warning about it on Johnny Carson's "Tonight" show. She had previously described it in detail to Mr. Haley and Dr. Riesenman. On November 1 the Soviet Union launched an unmanned satellite called Polyot 1, which made a series of orbit-changing maneuvers on radio signal from the earth. Soviet announcements described its "complex figures" in space, and a Russian armed forces publication said: "Our new maneuverable space ship, heeding radio commands from the earth, obediently turned first to one side, then to the other, soared up and dived, changing its position in space." This sounded eerily like the satellite that Jeane had foreseen.

On January 28, 1964, Americans learned that one of our T39 planes had been downed in East Germany. The three-man crew was dead. After an investigation the Air Force announced: "It is apparent that the T39 was experiencing communications difficulties, since it did not respond to any radio communication after 1430 o'clock, and that it was also having navigational difficulties. Obviously the pilot was unaware that he had strayed into the Soviet zone."

Could this communications failure have resulted from a strange new device such as Jeane had foreseen five months before? I do not know, but less than two months later one of our IB66 planes was also brought down in East Germany. This time the Air Force merely announced that the plane had "entered East Germany through navigational error," that an unidentified fighter had made a pass at it, and the impact occurred without warning. Because of our cold war with the Communist world, the mysterious straying of U.S. planes into enemy territory is a highly classified subject, and the true facts may not be revealed for many years. Astronautical attorney Haley says: "If the Soviets have indeed found a way to reverse the electromagnetic field anything is possible, including a communications blackout for America and our planes such as Mrs. Dixon foretells."

Never before revealed are several provocative occurrences which may or may not be significant. The first was in 1953, two days following Jeane's televised forecast about the first Russian satellite. She was working at her desk in the realty office when a man telephoned and in accented English asked if she could come to the Russian Embassy to see the ambassador.

Aware that the Soviets were shopping for real estate, she assumed that the call concerned business and took a cab to the embassy. Two men met her at the door of the former Pullman mansion, and one of them led her into an office to the left of the foyer. He spoke briefly on the intercom and then motioned her to precede him to the second floor. Ambassador Georgi Zaroubin was waiting to receive her in the drawing room. Her companion withdrew, leaving them alone. A servant entered with a tray of coffee, then departed. The ambassador, after pouring the thick beverage into demitasse cups, made a few casual remarks about their real estate problems. Leaning forward in his chair, he then smiled and said: "Mrs. Dixon, I had the pleasure of hearing your broadcast the other evening with Ambassador Davies. Tell me, where did you learn such information about a Russian space program? Where did you get the idea that we are going to have a—what you say—satellite?"

Jeane, who is as guileless as a child, replied that she had received no information "from anyone except God" but had been shown the vision while appearing on television.

Ambassador Zaroubin listened courteously. When she had completed her description of the vision he said: "Then you know something that we don't know. Our country is doing nothing like that."

Looking back to that day, Jeane muses: "He seemed genuinely puzzled and rather nonplused. I had the feeling that he knew something he did not wish to divulge, but that he was not quite sure what he himself knew."

A second incident took place the morning after her appearance on Johnny Carson's television show ten years later. An official from the Pentagon called, identified himself by name, and asked where she had secured her information about a Soviet satellite that could immobilize our communications. Brushing aside her explanation about the vision, he insisted on knowing the "real" source of her information. Somewhat offended by his brusque manner, Jeane replied: "My source is the same source which is available to all of us. Just reach up to God, and you shall receive."

A short time later former Congresswoman Coya Knutson telephoned from her Civilian Defense office in the Pentagon to say: "Jeane, you've got this building turned upside down. Everyone over here wants to know where you got your information for the Johnny Carson show last night."

Jeane told her that it was really quite simple and that she had tried to explain it to the Pentagon official who called earlier. "Now let me explain it the same way to you, Coya," Jeane began. "Pick up an inkwell and turn it clockwise in your hand. Everything is bright. Now, suddenly turn it counterclockwise and visualize everything going dark. That's the way this Russian satellite will operate. As it turns it blacks out our communications and lighting systems. I saw it happen in a vision." Mrs. Knutson knew better than to argue with Jeane. Scientifically trained Pentagon officials might not understand what her friend was talking about, but she herself had witnessed enough of Jeane's seeming miracles to accept them at face value.

The following day Jeane was working at her desk when the receptionist told her that "a man with a badge" was waiting to see her. He was only two steps behind the flustered woman. Identifying himself as an agent of one of our supersecret intelligence services, he asked if there was somewhere that they could talk in complete privacy. Jeane ushered him across the hall to the John Philip Sousa library, and as soon as the door closed behind them he asked where she had obtained the information for her broadcast. A bit wearily Jeane again recounted the vision which had appeared to her a few weeks before.

"But this is top secret," he expostulated. "You're not supposed to know about these things."

The devout woman had had enough. Tilting her chin, she retorted: "The Bible says, 'Ask and ye shall receive.' I ask God to show me anything which I should be able to tell others for the enlightenment and betterment of mankind. I think that He is the best judge of what I should know." The chastened agent thanked her and departed.

A few days later Coya Knutson told Senator Hubert Humphrey about Jeane's forecast concerning a Russian satellite that could knock out our communications. Coya says that Humphrey replied: "We have been fearful of just such a development for some time."

CHAPTER
17

THE sudden Kremlin shake-up in October 1964 took government officials here and abroad by complete surprise. The same could not be said of Jeane Dixon, however, who had predicted the previous December that Nikita Khrushchev would shortly be deposed. For my 1964 New Year's column she had written: "I foresee great danger in both domestic and foreign affairs for the United States during 1964-67. This danger will be heightened by a new leader who will replace Chairman Nikita Khrushchev within the next eighteen months. This man's name begins with an *s*. He is the professorial, intellectual type and will be much harder for us to deal with than Khrushchev. He is already working with Soviet, Chinese, and German scientists to plot our destruction, but he will not succeed."

As the world now knows, Khrushchev's duties as Premier and Communist party boss were divided in October between Leonid Brezhnev and Alexei Kosygin. Kremlinologists immediately began speculating, however, that the two men would probably be only temporary custodians of Soviet power until a new strong man emerged. It was noted that

Mikhail S. Suslov delivered the key address at the Communist party Central Committee meeting which effected the shake-up, and also made the motion for Khrushchev's ouster. A top intelligence source described sixty-two-year-old Suslov to me as "one of the very few intellectuals in the Russian hierarchy; a man of the definitely professorial type."

A month after Khrushchev's downfall, another man whose name begins with *s* came to the center of the stage in the Kremlin. Aleksandr Schelepin, elevated to the party Presidium, simultaneously held membership in the party Secretariat and the Presidium of the Council of Ministers. These are the three most powerful ruling bodies of Russia, and the Washington *Post,* in commenting editorially on Schelepin's unexpected elevation, said: "In addition [to these three other powerful positions] he is in charge of the very powerful committee on party-state control and probably still has overall responsibility for the secret police. The concentration of such enormous power in the hands of one man is difficult to explain."

In due time we shall learn whether a man whose name begins with *s* (Suslov? Schelepin?) wins out in the Kremlin power struggle and takes over the reins from the two men who are now sharing Khrushchev's former duties.

The same day as the Kremlin shake-up the Red Chinese exploded their first nuclear bomb, and Jeane Dixon could once again have said, "I told you so," about a world-shaking event. In my New Year's column of her predictions for 1963 she warned that Communist China would soon become eligible for membership in the exclusive "Atomic Club." With the nuclear explosion in October 1964, Red China automatically joined Russia, Britain, France, and the United States as a nuclear power.

Another paragraph in Jeane's 1964 forecast column bears repeating. "During the coming year," she wrote, "England will increase its trade with Russia, and Germany and Russia will establish greater economic ties. The Berlin wall will come down, but probably not before the year's end." By the latter half of that year, West Berliners were being permitted to cross through the wall almost at will to visit East Berlin relatives. West Germany was actively promoting better relations with Russia, and in a syndicated column from London, dated November 19, 1964, Washington columnist Charles Bartlett cabled: "Britain's trade with the Communists appears destined to be a fly in the ointment of British-American relations. The new Labor government is moving quickly to expand this controversial commerce." He went on to report that Douglas Jay, president of Britain's Board of Trade, flew to Moscow and Peking almost as soon as he took office in October, and reported to the House of Commons: "We must not neglect the opportunities, such as they are. I am determined to increase Russian purchases in Britain."

As has been her custom with almost monotonous regularity since she was a small child, with the possible exception of 1960, Jeane Dixon correctly picked the winner in the 1964 presidential race. She forecast in my column ten months beforehand that the Democratic slate would win. She did not foresee the landslide proportions of the victory, however, and mistakenly forecast that Britain's Conservative party would win by "a small majority," whereas it was the Labor party that won with a hair-thin majority.

Concerned that she might have misinterpreted the symbols in her crystal ball, Jeane discussed her perplexity with Dr. Riesenman, a psychiatrist. After listening to her recital, he told me that St. Thomas Aquinas had provided the answer more than seven hundred years earlier. Quoting the thirteenth-century theologian of the Roman Catholic Church, Dr. Riesenman said: "St. Thomas Aquinas theorized that there are two kinds of prophecies. One is given by God in visions, and is therefore inflexible. The other is subject to changing conditions which the prophet (in this case Mrs. Dixon) did not anticipate intellectually.

"In other words, the unsought visions which come to Mrs. Dixon are unchangeable, because they represent the will of God. The coming event cannot, consequently, be prevented. In this category I would place her vision of the assassination of President Kennedy. In the crystal ball, however, she seeks knowledge of coming events, and although her symbols reflect the situation at the time, such events are subject to change because of changing human conditions. Therefore, when she consulted her crystal ball in December 1963 the landslide proportions of President Johnson's victory did not exist. They were later to be man-made. Likewise, the British Conservatives were probably slightly ahead of the Labor party in public sentiment at the time that Mrs. Dixon saw them squeaking through."

Dr. Riesenman referred me to the *International Journal of Parapsychology* (Vol. VI, No. 4, pp. 389-407), 1964, for further enlightenment on prophecies. In an article, written by Renée Haynes, the onetime agnostic who became a Catholic convert in 1942 sought to explain Catholic saints in relation to the phenomenon of extrasensory perception (ESP). She quoted St. Thomas Aquinas as having written in the thirteenth century: "A vision of future events (an authoritative prophecy) is a direct influence from God."

She also cited the view of Pope Benedict, who became an authority on psychic phenomena after serving as a celebrated devil's advocate on the subject during the eighteenth century: "Visions are an inner knowing."

Father Alois Wiesinger, a priest of the Trappist order, writing on occult phenomena in 1959, traced visions to "the original spirituality of the soul before the fall." He said this power "still exists in latent dormant state in all of us" and "manifests itself spontaneously under certain conditions and situations."

Dr. Gebhard Free, a priest, has written of visions: "God so affects the soul that from it arises the appropriate pictures, words, and ideas." He and a fellow priest of the Society of Jesus related this pictures, words, and ideas to the visions seen by Pope Pius XII, St. John of the Cross, and the children of Fátima.

Speaking of Jeane Dixon and her precognitive powers, Dr. Riesenman declares: "Her visions come in on the highest channel of any seer or psychic whose work I have ever investigated. This includes the case studies I have made of many such gifted persons who have lived during the past three hundred years. I would rate Mrs. Dixon's visions and spiritual powers even higher than those of Emanuel Swedenborg. Swedenborg saw fires at a remote distance and was able to locate lost articles in supernatural ways, but there is no proof of his reported visions concerning heaven and hell. This could have been his own subconscious at work. By contrast Mrs. Dixon foresees births, deaths, and world-shaking events of historical significance, and proof of these is readily available."

(Swedenborg was the eighteenth-century Swedish scientist who in his later years developed such amazing psychic powers that a Swedenborgian church was founded to carry forward his work.)

Dr. Riesenman concludes: "I consider Mrs. Dixon to be an extraordinarily saintly person. In my investigations of her remarkable talents, she has no living peer."

CHAPTER
18

JEANE believes that she is an instrument of God, but only to the same degree as all others who try to use the talents with which they are blessed. She attempts to define her own philosophy of living in these terms: "It seems to me that we have a purpose in life. We came from God and we return to God. He would not be all-loving and all-merciful if He had not given us the means, at the time of our creation, also to return to Him. Each of us must therefore find and develop that purpose within ourselves. The talents with which we are born are the means for fulfilling our mission in life. They were intended not only to enrich our own lives but to help others. We are the stewards of a precious possession—our talents—and as in the biblical parable, we must invest them in such a way that we can return them to God with interest."

She is referring, of course, to Christ's parable about the man preparing to travel abroad who gave to one servant five talents, to another two, and to the third, one. On his return the master rewarded the two servants who had doubled their talents through wise investment, but on learning that the third servant had buried his lone talent, he was angered and took even that one from him.

"Our talents are intended to earn interest, not to lie dormant," Jeane emphasizes. "They have a purpose, and they must be used if we are to escape the punishment meted out to the hoarding servant. We are not to give back to God only what He gave us at birth. The potential is there. We are to utilize it. His kingdom exists for those who work for Him, and the reward is eternal. By employing these God-given talents to the fullest extent possible, we are truly able to say, 'My cup runneth over.'"

Jeane is concerned by the frequency with which people ask her: "What do you see for me?" Instead of seeking assurance that they will achieve security, fame, or fortune, she feels that they should be wondering: "What ought I to do with my life to fulfill God's will?" She refuses to tell people what they "want" to hear. Through her psychic gift she is often able to sense an individual's innate talents, and thereby to urge him to develop them; but the importance of this discovery, she feels, is measured by his realization that whatever talent he has is bestowed by his Creator to be utilized. "It is when we use these talents that we are doing His work upon this earth and fulfilling our purpose in life," she stresses. "To live for God's greater glory is to work with the tools that He has given us."

In Jeane's opinion, anyone can discover his own specific talents through faith and prayer. "Faith in our Creator," she says, "should be the foundation of our lives, upon which we work and build. If we could do only what we want to, we might all be millionaires, doing nothing but sailing on yachts and living in palaces. But that is not God's plan. Who then would take care of the yacht and clean the palace for us? God has a vineyard to be kept; a universe to run. Each of us has our place in helping with this operation.

"If we all did the same thing, how dull the world would be! Fortunately we have been assigned different talents. Some of us are called to preach, others to teach, and some to work

in the fields. We should never be jealous or envious of another's gift or talent, for then we cannot be free within ourselves. We cannot be free when we hold hatred. The forces
for good and evil are in all of us, but we must learn to free
ourselves of the chains of malice and the longing for material
things. We are all created equal in the eyes of God, but we
are endowed with varying degrees of intelligence, social
status, and possessions. These God-given gifts carry corre-
sponding responsibilities—responsibilities that we must meet
with love in our hearts and gratitude for being given an
opportunity to serve."

Jeane believes that each day should begin with prayer. We
should, she insists, "pray as though everything depended
upon God; then, with His inspiration and love, go forth to
work as though everything depended upon us." She visualizes
an ideal community, governed by men of true spirituality, in
which "giving rather than getting" would be the mark of a
successful life. In such a community a person's worth would
not be determined by whether he or she is a king, queen,
bricklayer, teacher, executive, or laborer, but rather according to the "fullness with which we utilize our talents in service for others." We would be concerned less with self-will
and more with God's will.

She disagrees with those who speak of a person's environ-
ment as "an accident of birth." She believes there is no accident; that each of us is an integral part of God's over-all plan.
Elucidating this philosophy, she says: "He has a very special
duty for each and every one of us. God works in mysterious
ways His wonders to perform. When we accept this great
master plan, we realize that each of us has the same opportunity to develop according to God's will, regardless of color,
nationality, or station in life. Each of us is a member of the
human race, and what we do as human beings is far more important than how we develop socially or economically. Man

may owe allegiance to a particular religion, nation, political party, class, or race, but he has the God-given ability to think and to love. Respect is what we owe; love is what we give.

"The Bible says: 'To everything there is a season, and a time for every purpose under the sun.' That purpose is the realization of our talents. Christ said: 'Greater love hath no man than this, that he lay down his life for a friend.' That is love in the true sense. If we use our talents to help others, we are fulfilling our mission in life. Faith alone is not enough, but faith combined with deeds can surmount any obstacle."

Jeane views her own strange ability to glimpse future events as a gift entrusted to her by God, just as is any other talent. "I believe that I am only an instrument through which these things come, for a purpose," she says. "I go to church every morning, and I pray as though everything depends on God. Then I work as though it all depends on me. I ask for divine guidance and wisdom, but I try to use the intellect that He has given me."

Asked whether her gift sometimes weighs heavily on her shoulders, she replied simply: "No, it doesn't, because I believe that I have been given a job to do. The only time that I was really upset for an extended period was when I foresaw the assassination of President Kennedy and was unable to prevent it, even though I desperately tried to do so. Perhaps that was my mistake, because the will of humanity cannot change the will of God. We must learn that things are to be done in His time, not our time." To illustrate, she mentioned that an important man calls her frequently to complain that he "prays and prays," but nothing happens. "I tell him to start praying for others and forget about himself." She shrugs. "Lose yourself, and things will come in His timing. We must work and have patience. We must believe that each of us is His representative upon this earth, and that we are doing the job He has given us to do, by developing our talents and using our intelligence."

She recalls writing a letter to the chief of police, pra
an officer with Badge Number 428 who directed traffic o'
street corner near her office. The next time she saw Chiei
Robert V. Murray, she asked if he had received her letter,
and he replied: "Yours is only one of hundreds of commendations that I have had about this officer, whose name,
incidentally is John W. Harrison." Jeane asked why he did
not give the man a promotion, and the chief replied: "Because he loves it where he is and wants to stay there."

"This officer is a Negro," Jeane says, "but whenever I pass
that corner I pick up his vibrations, which are as wonderful
as those of any leader I have ever met. In the eyes of God, I
feel sure that his gift is as great as was General Douglas Mac-
Arthur's, President Johnson's, President de Gaulle's, or a
kindly taxi driver's. He is doing God's work as surely as any
one of them."

Jeane is convinced that her own gift is no more remarkable
than that of the Negro policeman who has earned so many
unsought commendations. St. Paul described this elusive
quality when, in the twelfth and thirteenth chapters of First
Corinthians, he wrote: "But the manifestation of the Spirit is
given to every man to profit withal. For to one is given by the
Spirit the word of wisdom; to another the word of knowledge
by the same Spirit; to another faith by the same Spirit; to
another the gifts of healing by the same Spirit; to another the
working of miracles; to another prophecy; to another discern-
ing of spirits; to another divers kinds of tongues; to another
the interpretation of tongues."

St. Paul compared these various talents to the separate
parts of the body which work together to form the whole
man. "And God hath set some in the church; first apostles,
secondarily prophets, thirdly teachers, after that miracles,
then gifts of healing, helps, governments, diversities of
tongues," he continued, but sounded this warning: "Though
I speak with the tongues of men and of angels, and have not

...he as sounding brass, or a tinkling cymbal.
...e the gift of prophecy, and understand all
...knowledge; and though I have all faith, so
...iove mountains, and have not charity, I am

..., Jeane places her own greatest emphasis on
...elping others without expectation of reward.
Perhaps she best expressed her personal philosophy the day
that the young teen-ager whom she had befriended asked how
she could repay her, and Jeane replied: "If a person helps
someone else, and then that person helps another, it sets up a
chain reaction. All I ever ask of you is that if the opportunity
arises and you are able, you will help someone else in need. I
want no other thanks."

Those who bemoan their fate, instead of accepting the
hard bumps and pressing onward, can expect little sympathy
from Jeane. Thoughtfully assessing the seeming inequality of
man's lot, she says: "Those with the greatest burdens may be
the most blessed, if they recognize the challenge of the
burdens. The richness of joy is somehow in direct proportion
to the experience of suffering. Each of us has known a sense
of achievement, and the depth of that sense has been influenced by the failures we have known. Before the blooms appear so hopefully in spring, the barren winter must come. If,
therefore, we believe that there is a power in us which we can
put to use when the need is clear, then the greater the obstacle, the greater the blessing. Call it what you will, but it
brings out the best in us to overcome the obstacles of life."

Anxious to make herself clear on her deeply felt view of
the importance of talents, she furrowed her brow for a moment and then continued: "Our talents are our weapons for
security and survival—eternal survival. Think of the porcu-
pine. Just as the Lord equipped him with sharp little needles
that he can throw at others to protect himself, so God gave us
talents in order to fulfill our mission in life."

Lifting her blue-green eyes, which seem to look into one's heart, she summarized: "There are plateaus to achievement in everyone's life—pauses when we can stop briefly to reassess our progress—but there is no end to what anyone can accomplish."

Jeane Dixon is a living testament to her own philosophy.

CHAPTER
19

JEANE has won international renown as a crystal-gazer. Less well known is the fact that some of her more remarkable unfoldments have been revealed by unsought visions. Since early childhood she has grown accustomed to odd glimpses of tomorrow, but four distinct visions experienced in recent years fit into a mosaic which Jeane believes has enormous significance for all mankind.

The first of these seemingly momentous visions occurred shortly after midnight on July 14, 1952. Without it, she feels, she would not have been able to interpret the more enlightening visions that were to follow. Washington is humid in midsummer, and Jeane had only a sheet across her body as she lay in bed. She was drowsy but not asleep.

"Suddenly I could feel a physical motion against the mattress, to the left of my head," she recounts. "I rolled onto my left side, facing the east, and as I did so I saw the body of a snake. It was no bigger around than a garden hose, and I could see neither its head nor its tail. I felt its powerful little body twisting down the side of my bed and raising the corner of the mattress at the foot. Then, though I seemed cloaked in a substance as soft as eiderdown, I could feel its head nudging beneath my ankles, and its body growing larger as it wrapped itself around my legs and hips.

"I was not frightened. I knew instinctively that I was to be shown how little I understood about life. As the snake gradually entwined itself around my chest I could see its head but not its eyes. They were gazing toward the east, rather than at me. By this time the snake was as big around as a man's arm. While I watched, it slowly turned its eyes and gazed into mine. In them was the all-knowing wisdom of the ages. Although the room had been in almost total darkness, it was now bathed in brilliant light. The snake, vividly colored in yellow and black, had great jowls shaped like miniature pyramids. It did not speak, but I seemed to know that it was telling me that I had much, much to learn.

"It turned its head, looking again to the east and then at me, as if to say that I too must look to the east for God's wisdom and guidance. I sensed that it was telling me that if my faith was great enough I could penetrate some of this divine wisdom. I knew that I had God's protection, for the steady gaze of the reptile was permeated with love, goodness, strength, and knowledge. A sense of 'peace on earth, good will toward men' coursed through my being. I had a feeling of suspension and yet of tremendous stability. A purplish ray led from the bed to the window at the east, and as I watched, the snake gradually withdrew toward my feet. As silently as it came it left the bed and vanished to the right. I interpreted this to mean that we must look to the east for growth and to the west for the ending of things. The brilliant illumination faded and it was dark again in the room. I looked at the radium dial on my bedside clock. The time was 3:14 A.M."

Jeane says that for three days before the eerie experience she had "felt something coming on" but did not know what to expect. "Seven is a miracle number," she explains. "When I receive important visions they invariably occur on the

⌐⌐

er this sense of unreality overtakes me. Another
e required for the spell to vanish. There is no
ly to describe the sensation to someone who has
ced it, but it comes as near to perfect oneness
can be felt in this world. Love for all humanity
floods the heart and soul. You want to help everyone."

Jeane believes that the purpose of this vision was to prepare her for three others which seem closely interlinked and
are of a deeply spiritual nature. The second occurred on a
blustery, rainy weekday morning in 1958. She had entered St.
Matthew's Cathedral for prayers and meditation. Choosing
ten purple containers, she was preparing to burn candles for
intentions, and had reached into her purse for coins when she
found her hands entangled in a mass of purple and gold balls.
As she gazed in awe, the small balls floated upward and gradually merged into a massive purple disk edged in gold. It
encircled the knees of the statue of the Virgin Mary, rising
gently until it enveloped her breast and head, like an up-
tilted halo.

"The Holy Mother's face came alive," Jeane reverently
recounts, "and the most magnificent sunshine that I had ever
seen flooded down from the dome of the church. It was a
dark, stormy morning outside and the church was virtually
empty, but suddenly brilliant rays shone on every imaginable
people and religion. The cathedral overflowed with peasants
in babushkas, kings and queens in royal raiment, the rich and
poor of every nationality and creed. I could not see a single
vacant pew. Everyone was bathed in the same sunshine, and I
seemed to be standing on something as soft as new-fallen
snow. A remarkable peace overcame me, and I knew that a
council of our Church would soon bring together under the
roof of the Holy See in Rome the religions and nationalities
of all the world."

The vision slowly faded, but the memory remained vivid.
When Jeane went to her office she immediately sought out

Shirley Peick, her part-time secretary, who is a Roman Catholic convert. Mrs. Peick recalls that Jeane was "literally glowing" as she described the vision that had come to her that rainy morning. "Our Church is going to call a great council of all the faiths and creeds," Jeane told her. "Peoples from every land will be represented, and eventually all religions will be brought together under one sun. Our Holy See in Rome is going to start the trend."

Less than four years after Jeane's vision in St. Matthew's Cathedral, Pope John XXIII summoned an Ecumenical Council of the Roman Catholic Church in Rome, the second ever to have been held in St. Peter's Basilica. Twenty-seven hundred high prelates attended, making it the greatest gathering of the Roman Catholic hierarchy in history. In attendance also as delegate-observers were twenty-eight non-Catholic prelates, representatives of most major Protestant denominations; and dignitaries from the Eastern Orthodox Church of the Middle East and of the Russian Orthodox Church. The following September the Ecumenical Council reconvened with twenty-five hundred ecclesiastical dignitaries and fifty observers from non-Catholic denominations. Pope Paul VI, in his opening discourse, made an appeal for Christian unity and stated that the long-range goal of the Council was the complete and universal union of all Christians.

Shirley Peick says that the moment she heard of Pope John's call for an Ecumenical Council she remembered her former employer's prophecy and told her husband: "This is what Jeane's vision foretold."

Jeane herself believed that the vision foreshadowing the unprecedented Ecumenical Council was a mere first step in her awakening knowledge of the future of religion. The next step came near the close of that year, while she was kneeling at prayer in St. Matthew's Cathedral and holding in her hands a crystal ball. In hushed tones Jeane recalls: "Suddenly the very air seemed rarefied. A glorious light shown again from the dome of the cathedral, and before me stood the Holy Mother. She was draped in purplish blue and surrounded by gold and white rays which formed a halo of light around her entire person.

"In a cloudlike formation to the right and just above her I read the word 'Fátima' and sensed that the long-secret prophecy of Fátima was to be revealed to me. I saw the throne of the Pope, but it was empty. Off to one side I was shown a Pope with blood running down his face and dripping over his left shoulder. Green leaves of knowledge showered down from above, expanding as they fell. I saw hands reaching out for the throne, but no one sat in it, so I realized that within this century a Pope will be bodily harmed. When this occurs, the head of the Church will thereafter have a different insignia than that of the Pope. Because the unearthly light continued to shine so brightly on the papal throne, I knew that power would still be there but that it would not rest in the person of a Pope. Instead, the Catholic Church would blaze the trail for all peoples of every religion to discover the meaning of the Almighty Power; to grow in wisdom and knowledge. This, I feel sure, was the prophecy of Fátima."

Those familiar with the miracle of Fátima will recall the story of Lucia dos Santos and her cousins, Jacinta and Francisco Marto. On May 13, 1917, the three Portuguese children saw their first vision of the Virgin Mary in the bleak hill country of Fátima. During a series of visitations thereafter, Our Lady gave the children a number of prophecies concerning the two World Wars and Russia. On the day of her sixth appearance in October, when the Virgin had promised a miracle, seventy thousand people traveled through a downpour to reach Fátima. At noon the rains stopped, the sun burst through, and at Lucia's cry that the Lady had come, a celestial display stunned the awe-struck viewers. Three times the solar disc spun in the sky, then plunged downward, but gradually resumed its proper place high in the heavens. Even the skeptics had to concede that something had interfered with normal cosmic law. The prophecies revealed by the children before the untimely deaths of Jacinta and Francisco came to pass. Lucia joined a convent, and in 1927 she reported that Christ had appeared before her and asked that one of his prophecies be kept secret until 1960. Sister Lucy sealed it in an envelope and reportedly conveyed it through church intermediaries to the Pope in Rome.

Catholics the world over eagerly awaited revelation of the prophecy, and in 1960 Catholic information centers were swamped with inquiries. For some reason unknown to laymen, it has not yet been revealed. Jeane believes that the vision she saw at the end of 1958, foretelling the close of the papal reign of the Church within this century, was the same as the "prophecy of Fátima." She feels that its full meaning was not disclosed to her, however, until more than three years later.

The vision which Jeane considers to be the most significant and soul-stirring of her life occurred shortly before sunrise on February 5, 1962. The date itself may have special significance, though Jeane was unaware of that fact at the time. For several months beforehand astrologers and soothsayers had been predicting an earth-shaking event on that day—some even forecast the end of the world—because of a rare conjunction of the planets. A similar conjunction which occurred nearly two thousand years ago is believed by some biblical scholars to explain the "bright star in the east" which dazzled shepherds and guided three Wise Men to a humble manger behind a crowded inn in Bethlehem.

Three nights before Jeane's vision she was meditating in her room when she became aware that the light was dimming. Glancing up, she saw the five bulbs in the crystal chandelier go dark, except for a curious round ball which

iantly in the center of each. Strangely frightened,
her husband's bedroom and told him of the light
e their other house lights were working properly,
ssumed that a fuse for one circuit had blown, but
when he started down the hall to investigate he noticed that
Jeane's chandelier was again burning brightly.

The next evening during her meditations the phenomenon recurred. This time Jeane remained quietly in her
room, staring at the tiny balls of light in the otherwise dark-
ened bulbs. In approximately ten seconds, she says, she heard
"a tiny crackling sound." The wires in the clear bulbs then
began to glow again, and normal light resumed. When the
performance was repeated exactly as before on the third evening, Jeane accepted it as an omen that something important
was soon to befall. She did not know when or where. The
next morning she overslept, but the sun was not yet up as she
walked toward the bay window of her bedroom, which faces
east.

As she gazed outside she saw, not the bare-limbed trees and
city street below, but a bright blue sky above a barren desert.
Just above the horizon was the brightest sun that she had ever
seen, glowing like a golden ball. Splashing from the orb in
every direction were brilliant rays which seemed to be drawing the earth toward it like a magnet. Stepping out of the
brightness of the sun's rays, hand in hand, were a Pharaoh
and Queen Nefertiti. Cradled in the Queen's other arm was a
baby, his ragged, soiled clothing in startling contrast to the
gorgeously arrayed royal couple. "The eyes of this child were
all-knowing," Jeane says softly. "They were full of wisdom
and knowledge."

A little to one side of Queen Nefertiti, Jeane could glimpse
a pyramid. While she watched entranced, the couple advanced
toward her and thrust forth the baby, as if offering it to
the entire world. Within the ball of the sun, Jeane saw Joseph guiding the tableau like a puppeteer pulling strings.

Now, rays of light burst forth from the baby, blending with those of the sun and obliterating the Pharaoh from her sight. Off to the left, she observed that Queen Nefertiti was walking away, "thousands of miles into the past." The Queen paused beside a large brown water jug, and as she stooped and cupped her hands to drink she was stabbed in the back by a dagger. Jeane says that she "distinctly heard her death scream as she vanished."

Jeane shifted her gaze back to the baby. He had by now grown to manhood, and a small cross which formed above him began to expand until it "dripped over the earth in all directions. Simultaneously, peoples of every race, religion, and color (black, yellow, red, brown and white), each kneeling and lifting his arms in worshipful adoration, surrounded him. They were all as one." Unlike previous visions, which had gradually faded away from Jeane, this one moved ever nearer until she seemed to be in the very midst of the action, joining in the adoring worship. "I felt like a tiny seed ready to sprout and grow," she says, "but I was only one of millions of similar seeds. I knew within my heart, 'Here is the beginning of wisdom.' " The room was becoming dark again, and though she was still caught up in the spell of the vision, Jeane glanced automatically at her bedside clock. The time was 7:17 A.M.

What does it mean? What is the significance of this strange visitation on a dull February morning in Washington, a third of the way around the world from Egypt? Jeane feels that she has been shown that answer. A bit haltingly, she explains it this way: "A child, born somewhere in the Middle East shortly after 7 A.M. (EST) on February 5, 1962, will revolutionize the world. Before the close of the century he will bring together all mankind in one all-embracing faith. This will be the foundation of a new Christianity, with every sect and creed united through this man who will walk among the people to spread the wisdom of the Almighty Power.

"This person, though born of humble peasant origin, is a descendant of Queen Nefertiti and her Pharaoh husband; of this I am sure. There was nothing kingly about his coming— no kings or shepherds to do homage to this newborn baby— but he is the answer to the prayers of a troubled world. Mankind will begin to feel the great force of this man in the early 1980's, and during the subsequent ten years the world as we know it will be reshaped and revamped into one without wars or suffering. His power will grow greatly until 1999, at which time the peoples of this earth will probably discover the full meaning of the vision."

Attempting to describe her own sensation, Jeane says: "I felt suspended and enfolded, as if I were surrounded by whipped cream. For the first time I understood the full meaning of the biblical phrase, 'My cup runneth over.' I loved all mankind. I felt that I would never again need food or sleep, because I had experienced perfect peace."

As a reporter, I felt there were questions that must be asked. How could she be sure that the queen in her vision was Nefertiti? Who was the Pharaoh who disappeared back into the sun? Why was Joseph in the vision? Jeane could answer only in part. She said that she recognized Nefertiti from a small bust of the famed Egyptian Queen, which a friend once brought to her from Cairo. She "knew" that the Pharaoh was married to Nefertiti but had no idea of his name or identity. Joseph seemed to be controlling the couple and inducing them to present the child to the world, but she did not know why.

Baffled by the meaning of the strangely compelling vision, I consulted the Old Testament to jog my memory about Joseph. I recalled, of course, that as the favorite son of Jacob he had been sold into Egyptian bondage by jealous older brothers. I knew that eventually he saved his family from starvation, when famine came, but beyond that . . . what? Turning to Genesis, I read that "hidden things were revealed to him" and he was able to "interpret dreams." Because of this, a grateful Pharaoh made him governor of all Egypt and presented him with a wife, Asenath, whose father Potipherah was an influential priest.

So Joseph could understand hidden meanings and interpret dreams! I next turned to the Encyclopædia Britannica and learned that Nefertiti was the wife of Pharaoh Amenhotep IV who, after abandoning the worship of Amon, "devoted himself to that of the Aton (the solar disk)." He thereafter changed his name to Ikhnaton and built a new capital dedicated to worship of the sun on the banks of the Nile above Cairo. Archaeological evidence suggested that Nefertiti was also an "ardent supporter of the Aton (sun worship) religion." They had seven daughters but no sons. Suddenly I realized how strange it was that Jeane Dixon, who was totally unaware that Nefertiti and her husband had worshiped the sun, nevertheless "saw" them stepping forth from the solar disk in a vision.

CHAPTER
20

RECENT generations have marveled at the farsightedness of the Victorian poet, Alfred Tennyson, who wrote in *Locksley Hall:*

For I dipped into the future, far as human eye could see,
Saw the Vision of the world, and all the wonder that would be;
Saw the heavens fill with commerce, argosies of magic sails,
Pilots of the purple twilight, dropping down with costly bales;
Heard the heavens fill with shouting, and there rain'd a ghastly
    dew
From the nations' airy navies grappling in the central blue.
Far along the world-wide whisper of the southwind rushing
    warm,
With the standards of the peoples plunging through the
    thunderstorm;
Till the war drum throbbed no longer and the battle flags were
    furled
In the Parliament of man, the Federation of the world.

When these prophetic words were written in 1842 the airplane had yet to be invented; yet Tennyson seemingly foresaw the twentieth century's world commerce in air traffic, a rain of destruction such as that dropped from planes over Hiroshima and Nagasaki, and "nations' airy navies" fighting wars with bombers high above the earth. Who, then, can gainsay his further vision of a time when the roll of war drums will be silenced and peace will return through a Parliament of man?

Jeane Dixon foresees that this peace for which men long will dawn in the year 1999, but not before a world holocaust has shocked mankind into spiritual renewal. Some of her long-range predictions for the remainder of the century are these:

* Our two biggest headaches will be the racial problem and Red China. Through the latter's subversion and meddling in the racial strife, numerous African and Asian nations will turn against us and provoke a world war in the decade of the 1980s. Vietnam and Korea will lead us into this "inevitable" war with the Red Chinese.

* History will demonstrate that the test-ban treaty was bad for America and will be used against us. It is in our national interest to trade with Russia, although until the 1980s this trade will benefit the Kremlin more than us. Then will come a turning point, and we will align ourselves with Russia in the war against Red China.

* Red China will invade Russian territory, but this will be a border skirmish and will not ignite the later war to come, in which Red China will wage "germ warfare." In this period late in the century the Davis Straits will become an American "life line."

* American officials and scientists are mistakenly shelving "a baby missile which is approximately eighteen inches long, dark green or black in color, shaped like an elongated balloon." About 1970 this missile, which is small enough to be carried on a battlefield by two or three soldiers, will be critically needed for the protection of our country but will not be available. Two other missiles, "one shaped like a miniature

whale with two tiny fins, and another which explodes out of a pipelike instrument," should also be rushed to completion.

* Our foreign policy should be motivated by the desire to protect American interests, rather than by "some mysterious humanitarian ideal." We should not try to make over European nations in our own image, but rather accept the differences and work with them.

* Our space program should be accelerated, and parts of it which are now under civilian control should be transferred to the air force, where unprecedented progress could be made in protecting our security. Russia will be the first nation to put a man on the moon, probably in about three years' time.

* President Johnson is becoming "cognizant of the fact that there are some Communist sympathizers in our government" and will take steps at what he considers the appropriate time to eliminate them, but the action will come too late. This situation is not of his own making, since he inherited these officials.

* The years between 1964 and 1967 are a period of great national peril, in both the domestic and foreign fields. Mistakes will be made which may not be fully realized for a decade. America will have three Presidents in the period between 1961 and 1969.

* Great wisdom will flow from certain decisions made by Gamal Abdel Nasser, President of the United Arab Republic, and because of some alliances that he will forge.

* Pope Paul VI will leave the greatest imprint for good in the history of the papacy, but both he and President Lyndon B. Johnson are vulnerable to great personal danger.

* The President's program for the Great Society will fail, because the channels are running in all directions and none of the ends are closed. His War on Poverty will also fail unless more spirituality is introduced into the program, because "man does not live by bread alone, and it takes more than food and money to restore the dignity of man."

* During the next two decades we will move steadily downhill "in pride, accomplishments, and dignity," until the outbreak of war makes us realize our errors and inspires a program of reform.

* Sargent Shriver and Richard M. Nixon have "excellent vibrations" for the good of America and will serve their country well. The former, however, must guard against assassination attempts.

* The principles of Barry Goldwater will be vindicated, and despite his overwhelming defeat at the polls great honors will be showered upon him within twenty years. He will come to be venerated to an even greater degree than was the late Herbert Hoover, who was falsely castigated for the Great Depression but lived to become a revered elder statesman.

* The Republican party will be victorious at the polls in 1968, but within the following decade the two-party system as we have known it will vanish from the American scene.

Jeane Dixon has learned by experience that the early hours before daybreak provide the clearest channels for psychic meditation. She consequently arose at two o'clock on the morning of November 2, 1964, to meditate on the following day's election returns. She was disturbed that in recent weeks the elephant had disappeared from her crystal ball; only the donkey remained, tugging and pulling its way through dark clouds. Since this had never previously happened in all the years that she had been forecasting election outcomes, she hoped to find an explanation for the puzzlement. The street lights cast a wan yellow glow through her bedroom windows as she settled herself in the semidarkness, with the crystal ball in hand. The donkey was still there, pushing its nose against the finish line, but where was the Republican elephant? So intent was she on the little tableau in the glittering ball that she was only vaguely aware of an odd sensation of suspension, until she glanced toward the east and "saw a magnificent marble pavilion."

Jeane describes the vision thus: Seated on a throne before fluted marble columns was a gorgeously arrayed Roman emperor who, with great energy and strength, was hurling bits of food toward far-off throngs of ragged barbarians. The hoards gradually inched closer, seizing on the scattered tidbits, while beauty radiated from the exquisite pavilion. Watching intently, Jeane noticed that the emperor was beginning to cast the food more carelessly, with less vitality, so that some of it was falling near his feet; and at last the barbarians swept across the pavilion like a swarm of locusts, eradicating all traces of the culture and refinement which it reflected.

As darkness enveloped the scene, Jeane felt that in a symbolic way she had not only witnessed the decline and fall of the Roman Empire, with the subsequent Dark Ages which obliterated the light of learning, but had also been given a subtle warning that America was similarly draining itself of needed strength by a careless disbursement of foreign aid.

While she sat in reverie a new vision began to form, and Jeane suddenly found herself in the center of it, talking with a recognizable friend, who seemed implicitly to trust her, and an enormous old woman who represented the Voice of Wisdom. Wildly victorious music flooded the room through open windows, and Jeane knew instinctively that an American presidential inauguration was in progress just outside. The friend tenderly handed her a baby girl, saying: "I would trust her with no one but you. Please protect her, for I love her very much."

Nodding sagely, the old lady cautioned: "This is the child of love. You must let nothing happen to her." Jeane cuddled the infant in her arms, and as she left the house the door closed noiselessly behind her. She glanced in the direction from which the music had come, but the beautiful inaugural pavilion that had until recently been crowded with merry-makers was abandoned, and a filthy debris covered its smooth marble floor. The baby by now was a toddler, and Jeane held onto the tiny hand as she led her down a curving marble staircase.

She felt strangely drawn toward the pavilion, but since it was too soiled for the child to walk on, they strolled along beside it, on emerald-green grass which was as soft as velvet carpeting. Jeane seemed to realize that the marble pavilion was America, and she felt sick at heart that it had become so littered with filth. Now sparkling, pure, clear water was flowing across the grass and lapping gently around her ankles, but she sadly noted that the cleansing flood was sweeping under instead of over the debris on the pavilion floor.

The child happily trudging along beside her abruptly slipped into an unseen hole. Bracing herself against the pavilion for support, Jeane frantically tugged at the arm of the baby who had been so lovingly entrusted to her care, and as she struggled to lift her she beseeched the child: "Help me. Help me to save you. You can help me if you try."

The child made no effort to assist but slowly rolled over and gazed up at her; and though an inch of clear water covered the little face, Jeane knew that she had never seen such serenity, overwhelming love, and wisdom in human eyes. She continued her futile tugging until the child smiled and said joyously: "It must be this way. It's got to be this way. Don't you see that it must be this way?"

Jeane turned and stared again at the unspeakable litter covering the pavilion floor, and sensed that she belonged to it; that this was her America. Overwhelmed by a feeling of shame, she watched mutely while smoky gray clouds began to churn the debris about, like matchboxes caught in the funnel of a tornado. She lifted her eyes and noticed that above the murky clouds were even blacker ones, rolling in angry billows as if sucked by a giant magnet. As far as she could see.

the horizon was murky and tormented; but near the top of the black clouds a fire crackled and burned with white-hot intensity, gradually consuming the repulsive debris. Above the unearthly heat a gentle flame began to glow, and she saw with relief that the healing flame was spreading throughout the universe to disperse the fierce black clouds.

"This is the aura-flame, this is the aura-flame," a voice repeatedly told her, and slowly a blue tranquillity returned to the tortured sky. Glancing a little to the right, Jeane then beheld a beautiful green knoll on which glowed an eternal flame, and as the vision faded she realized that the knoll bore a marked resemblance to the Arlington hillside on which the mortal remains of John Fitzgerald Kennedy rest beside an eternal flame. In that instant she felt that she had been shown why President Kennedy's death was an integral part of God's plan; and why her warning of impending assassination was not meant to reach him, or to deter him from completing his preordained mission in life.

Jeane interprets this vision as an advance warning that Americans must pay dearly for "the confusion, degradation, and immorality in our political, business, labor, and family lives"; for our obsession with material things and our compromises with high principle. Like the Romans who squandered their great cultural and political leadership with bread and circuses, she feels that we also are building up a loathsome debris that must be consumed by cleansing fires before peace can return to a troubled world. Jeane says of this:

"I saw the debris of our national life littering America, but surrounding it was a sea of pure green grass which became inundated with sparkling clear water that still left the debris unswept. This was the present time, and as the gray clouds began to churn I knew that they represented the struggle between the races—a struggle that will dominate the decades of the 1960s and 1970s. After that came the even blacker clouds, representing a horrible war in which many Asian and

African nations whom we have helped with foreign aid will join with Red China to close in on us and, like the barbarians in the vision of ancient Rome, try to destroy our way of life. This will occur during the 1980s, and because of a new kind of germ warfare, many will die like ants.

"Then comes the aura-flame, like a vision of hope, to dispel the war clouds, and after that the eternal flame. This is the true meaning of President Kennedy's life and death: that through his martyrdom he would light an eternal flame to remind peoples of the world of God's eternal flame in each of us. During John Kennedy's brief period in the public spotlight, he was able to kindle in the hearts of men an awareness that there is more to life than the narrow pursuit of personal gain. Because his life on this earth was cut short in its prime, it was possible for him to become an eternal symbol of youth, vitality, culture, and intellect. This was not of his doing but of God's. Like the courteous Washington policeman on the street corner, who radiates good vibrations to all passers-by, and like each of us who tries to develop the talents that were entrusted to us, President Kennedy was simply an instrument of God's will. Through him God has demonstrated that within each of us burns this eternal flame; that our greatness lies not in the size of our bank accounts but in our faith and our development of divinely granted talents.

"We must realize our own talents and, having realized, accept them; and play on them like a symphony in which all other instruments are harmonized to make a better universe. I was wrong in trying to prevent the President's death, for nine years previously I had been shown that it was foreordained. The little toddler whom I tried to rescue in the vision taught me this great truth once again: that the will of humanity cannot change the will of God.

"How fortunate was John F. Kennedy to be chosen by our Lord for such a role! Like the little child who said, 'It must be this way,' he would not have wished his life or death to have been otherwise. This I know because of another vision which appeared before me on November 25, 1963, while I was watching his funeral on television. The President's casket was being carried out of St. Matthew's Cathedral—the same church in which I first saw the vision of his assassination in 1952—and as it was solemnly lifted into place on the caisson, I suddenly saw John Fitzgerald Kennedy dancing an Irish jig on top of it. He was happy and gay and free! The funeral procession moved slowly down the avenue, with the President continuing his merry twirling until it reached Memorial Bridge. At that juncture I saw Uncle Sam raise both his hands, as if pronouncing a benediction, and when I glanced back at the caisson only a fleecy trail of smoke remained where the President had danced."

On the green hillside directly opposite Memorial Bridge, an eternal flame now lights the grave of America's thirty-fifth President. Jeane Dixon believes that this symbolic torch can serve as an inspiration for those living during the holocaust which she foresees for the 1980s. After this period, she forecasts that Rome will once again become the world's foremost center of culture, learning, and religion; and that the Middle Eastern child whose birth she "witnessed in the vision with Queen Nefertiti" on February 5, 1962, will unite all warring creeds and sects into one all-embracing faith.

Mankind, Jeane Dixon has said, will begin to feel the great force of this man about 1980, and his power "will grow mightily" until 1999, when there will be "peace on earth to all men of good will."